Introduction to Test Construction in the Social and Behavioral Sciences

Introduction to Test Construction in the Social and Behavioral Sciences

A *Practical Guide*

Joshua A. Fishman and Tomás Galguera

ROWMAN & LITTLEFIELD PUBLISHERS, INC.
Lanham • Boulder • New York • Oxford

ROWMAN & LITTLEFIELD PUBLISHERS, INC.

Published in the United States of America
by Rowman & Littlefield Publishers, Inc.
A Member of the Rowman & Littlefield Publishing Group
4501 Forbes Boulevard, Suite 200, Lanham, Maryland 20706
www.rowmanlittlefield.com

PO Box 317
Oxford
OX2 9RU, UK

British Library Cataloguing in Publication Information Available

Library of Congress Cataloging-in-Publication Data

Fishman, Joshua A.
  Introduction to test construction in the social and behavioral
sciences : a practical guide / Joshua A. Fishman and Tomás Galguera.
    p. cm
Includes bibliographical references and index.
  ISBN 0-7425-2519-8 (alk. paper)—ISBN 0-7425-2520-1 (pbk. : alk.
paper)
  1. Psychological tests—Design and construction. I. Galguera, Tomás,
1960- II. Title.
  BF176 .F57 2003
  150'.28'7—dc21
                                                        2002152101

Printed in the United States of America

♾™ The paper used in this publication meets the minimum requirements of
American National Standard for Information Sciences—Permanence of Paper for
Printed Library Materials, ANSI/NISO Z39.48-1992.

To our students, on whose beards we learned to shave, and to our families, who, as always, waited patiently until we finished.

Contents

Tables and Figures		ix
Preface		xi
Introduction		1
Part A. Theoretical Topics		9
Chapter 1	What Are "Tests for Research Purposes"?	11
Chapter 2	The End Goal as a First Consideration	19
Chapter 3	Instrument Reliability	25
Chapter 4	Instrument Validity	35
Chapter 5	Item Analysis	51
Chapter 6	Sociopsychological Scales	69
Part B. Empirical Topics		77
Chapter 1	Designing Your Instrument: Componentiality and Item Type	81
Chapter 2	Preparation and Preliminary Testing of the First Version	91

Chapter 3	Analyzing Version 1: Item Statistics and Instrument Reliability	105
Chapter 4	Analyzing Version 2: Item Statistics, Instrument Reliability, and Validity	115
Chapter 5	Semiformal Measurement: Varieties of Content Analysis	127
Chapter 6	What Next? Back to the Future	135
Appendix A	Recommended Readings	141
Appendix B	Instructions for Performing Necessary Statistical Procedures in SPSS	143
Appendix C	Sample Data Set of Items and Scores for Self-Esteem Scale, Version 1	147
	References	159
	Index	161
	About the Authors	167

~

Tables and Figures

Tables

A4.1. Validity Analyses for Martin's Medical Coping Index,
Version 2 (MCI-2)   46

A4.2   Adachi's Multiple Linear Regression Scores for the
Criterion Level of Mean Distress by the Optimal Model
of Predictor Available with Caregiver Questionnaire,
Version 2 (CQ-2) Scores   47

A4.3. Adachi's Multiple Linear Regression Scores for the
Criterion Level of Mean Distress by the Optimal Model
of Predictor Available without Caregiver Questionnaire,
Version 2 (CQ-2) Scores   47

A6.1. Perfect and Less Than Perfect Item Scalability   75

B2.1. Martin's Items and Dimensions for the Medical Coping
Instrument, Version 1 (MCI-1)   99

B3.1. Perry's Decision Sheet for the Fear of Cancer
Self-Screening Instrument, Version 1 (FCSSI-1)   107

B3.2. Martin's Decision Sheet for Medical Coping Instrument,
Version 1 (MCI-1)   109

B3.3.   Items and Dimensions of Martin's Medical Coping
        Instrument, Version 2 (MCI-2)   111

B4.1.   Decision Sheet for Martin's Medical Coping Instrument,
        Version 2 (MCI-2)   120

B4.2.   Criterion Validity Analysis for Metcalf's English-Only
        in Government (EOG)   123

B5.1.   Four Kinds of Semiformal Measurement   129

Appendix C.1.
        Sample Data Set of Items and Scores for
        Self-Esteem Scale, Version 1   148

Figures

A5.1.   Perry's Item Difficulty Scores Distribution for the Fear of
        Cancer Self-Scrutiny Instrument, Version 1 (FCSSI-1)   55

A5.2.   Martin's Item Difficulty Scores Distribution for the
        Medical Coping Instrument, Version 1 (MCI-1)   57

A5.3.   Martin's Alpha-If-Item-Deleted Scores for the Mecial
        Coping Instrument, Version 1 (MCI-1)   59

A5.4.   Perry's Inter-Item Consistency Scores for the Fear of
        Cancer Self-Screening Instrument, Version 1 (FCSSI-1)   61

A5.5.   Martin's Item Discriminability Scores for the Medical
        Coping Instrument, Version 1 (MCI-1)   66

A5.6.   Perry's Item Discriminability Scores for the Fear of
        Cancer Self-Scrutiny Instrument, Version 1 (FCSSI-1)   67

B.1.   Item and Instrument Development, Analyses, and
        Refinement, Including Criterion Validity Assessment   79

B4.1.   Martin's Item Difficulty Scores Distribution for the
        Medical Coping Instrument, Version 2 (MCI-2)   117

B4.2.   Martin's Item Consistency Scores Distribution for
        Medical Coping Index, Version 2 (MCI-2)   118

B4.3.   Item Discriminability Scores for Martin's Medical
        Coping Index, Version 2 (MCI-2)   119

~

Preface

One of us (J.A.F.) has taught courses on test construction for research purposes for many years, on many campuses, and in diverse departments. Students in those courses typically were required to buy and read a well-known text in the field of testing. (See Recommended Readings list in Appendix A.) These texts tend to focus on tests that schools, hospitals, government offices, and businesses use as part of their normal operation and decision making processes. The relatively high-stakes associated with the use of such tests, such as whether or not to admit a student into a privileged university, administer a particular treatment to a patient, or hire and promote people, demand exacting standards from such instruments. Extensive resources and effort are devoted to ensure that operational tests of this kind yield scores that are expected to vary little if the same person took the test repeatedly. Care is also given to ensure that the questions or tasks used seem relevant to the decision to which the particular test is intended. However, the needs of budding researchers such as those enrolled in test construction courses are different from those of the aforementioned institutions. Researchers need instruments that will stand to scrutiny and gain acceptance by their respective research communities. Though the stakes surrounding research outcomes can be quite high for some researchers, the criteria for constructing tests for research purposes are clearly different from those involved in the construction of operational tests. Therefore, it was necessary to supplement the course reading materials with lectures on the specifics of test construction for research purposes. Largely, this book reflects the subjects covered in such lectures.

Before going any further, we would like to state that our use of the term "test" in this book reflects our concern for reliability and validity, particularly criterion validity, in research. Thus, we have chosen to be purposeful about using "test" instead of "quantitative instruments" or "questionnaires" because, as a research tool, tests provide a way to answer the questions, How do you know? And, How confident can you be about the explanation? Unfortunately we have seen too many "questionnaires" and "instruments" that, however thoughtfully they might have been created, offer neither answers to these questions nor ways to answer them. Not coincidentally, the authors of such research tools often are students such as those we work with. We will elaborate further on tests and formal and informal measurement in a subsequent chapter.

Largely because we understand the difficulties they face, we remain convinced that students planning to undertake research ought to familiarize themselves fully with the array of relevant, or partially relevant operational tests already available. They also need to be familiar with the special constraints and concerns particular to the makers of tests in general. Common principles and fundamental assumptions define most approaches to test construction. However, there are real and important differences between test construction for operational and research purposes. As such, it behooves students to become familiar with tests that are already available. It is also to their advantage to learn how to plan, construct, validate, and revise their own instruments for their own unique research purposes. Occasionally students may wish to use their own instruments in conjunction with or to supplement tests that are already available from test publishers, particularly since extensive descriptions and evaluations may be found in the professional literature.

This book is intended, therefore, for readers who need to go beyond the usual focus of texts on the use and evaluation of operational tests and develop their own tests for research purposes. Accordingly, we concentrate on both theoretical considerations and practical, empirical steps pertaining to the development of new measures for specific research purposes. Such new measures are constantly needed for the research purposes of investigators, whether working individually or in teams. This book is not intended to be a survey of test construction methods. Instead, we offer a practical approach to the construction of tests for research purposes for researchers with limited technical expertise. This book is also not directed at experts in test making or at researchers who are experienced in test design, development, and evaluation. Our intended audience includes both students in introductory research methods courses and independent researchers whose student experience might have ended years ago. We derive our approach from widely accepted notions and principles from the fields of statistics and test construction. We do not attempt to teach the reader statistical models or procedures, although we do include in our discussion basic statistical concepts (see "Prior Assumptions of this Text" in the introduction). Therefore, the organization of this text reflects these two general areas of concentration. We hope that by organizing the book in this manner, we facilitate its use either as a resource for a course on research methods or as a practical reference for researchers, particularly researchers with limited experience and resources. The tenor of this text, and of the courses from which it originated, is that reasonably good student-constructed tests for research purposes are clearly attainable. The experience of successfully creating and implementing a test for research purposes can be surprisingly enjoyable emotionally and a liberating experience intellectually. This is especially true for students who approach the endeavor with some initial trepidation because of an unfortunate impression that they are "no good at math" or "never liked statistics." In fact, students have often found that being good at or liking such matters often comes *after*, rather than before one is able to learn them. The experience is particularly rewarding to everyone learning skills and concepts in the motivationally powerful context of research that is both personally relevant and accessible.[1]

Note

1. We would like to express our gratitude to all of the classes who have contributed, directly and indirectly, to the conceptualization and preparation of this "user friendly" effort, and particularly, to the students whose work we cite. Specifically, we would like to thank Robert Manheimer and Stacey Weinberg, who went over the manuscript line-by-line. If it still doesn't achieve perfection (far from it!), its shortcomings are all ours, not theirs.

~

Introduction

The ideas behind the approach and rationale that we present in this book originate in a scientific tradition that is consonant with the history of testing. Science as a process depends on humans' ability to detect and observe ways in which phenomena manifest themselves in nature, even if this cannot always be done directly—as is often the case in the study of subatomic particles, for example. In other words, scientific findings must have an empirical basis. The scientific process also requires that, for an observation to count as empirical evidence, other scientists can agree on what is observed. As a community, scientists strive for objectivity, rather than individual subjectivity. Finally, the scientific process must also include measures that control for or eliminate, as much as possible, sources of confusion, bias, and error. Thus, researchers must strive toward empiricism, objectivity, and control as they design and develop experiments in subatomic physics or, in our case, tests to explain a social phenomenon. (See Singleton, Straits, and Straits 1998 for an elaboration on the foundations of social research.)

Keeping in mind the need for empiricism, objectivity, and control in scientific research, we take the position that external validity ought to be a fundamental concern in developing and using tests for research purposes. We believe that an instrument's validity ultimately resides in its ability to account for or explain an observable and measurable aspect of a phenomenon or phenomena (i.e., "the real thing"). Thus, it is essential that findings emerging from uses of tests for research purposes have clear

1

and direct empirical connections. The benefits of such an empirical bias are specially pertinent for emerging researchers who may lack the experience to distinguish between research findings that are either meaningful or noteworthy and those that are either research artifacts or minor. Hence, we recommend that in designing research that will depend on an instrument for data collection, researchers include a verifiable external criterion against which they may test their constructs as represented by their instruments. The latter must be constructed according to theoretical notions that contribute to the instrument's *internal* construct validity. Thereafter, it is incumbent upon researchers to demonstrate that the test has external validity as well.

Obviously alternatives exist to the approach our book represents. Many researchers, especially those embracing an ethnographic approach, would disagree with our ideas regarding the existence of a "real thing." Much ink and persuasive skills have been devoted to establishing whether one perspective is better than the other, especially in social research. As is often the case, the territory claimed by each camp varies by discipline and historical period.

In keeping with the practical tone of our book, we will not add to the debate beyond stating that one of the most appealing features of using tests for research is the promise of measuring the extent to which the test used explains what is being studied. In providing a way to estimate whether the variance for the external criterion may be explained by the variance in test scores, tests allow researchers to explain the relation between selected variables and an external, tangible, "real thing." We will expand on this notion in chapter A2 and A4. For those readers interested in an elaboration of the history and beliefs associated with other research traditions and ours, we refer them to the work of Tashakkori and Teddlie (1998).

Organization and Possible Uses

The organization of this book reflects our interest in making it as practical as possible to the reader. The first part, "Theoretical Topics," describes the conceptual framework for the method described in part B, "Empirical Topics." The reader will notice that the order of chapters in one section loosely parallels the order of chapters in the other. Our goal in organizing the chapters in such a way is to produce a book in which the procedure for developing and refining tests for research purposes stands alone, lending itself to be used almost as a manual. At the same time, we realize that the approach we describe needs a theoretical justification as well as a context to make it meaningful. Rather than attending to both goals simultaneously, we chose to keep them separate. We hope that in doing so we are being not only attentive to the needs of individual researchers who want quick access to specific practical information but also sensitive to instructors who want to teach both content and skills to students in research courses.

When used as reading material for a course, instructors will invariably differ as to how they utilize this text, depending not only on their instructional styles but also on the degree to which they wish to cover both operational tests and test construction for research purposes in a single course. We clearly emphasize the latter over the former (although the difference between them is often a matter of degree rather than of kind), primarily because we assume that most readers already are somewhat familiar with various operational tests and the basic principles of test administration and interpretation. Regardless of the book's organization, we recommend that the content in the two sections is taught in combination, weaving back and forth between theoretical and practical topics. The theoretical considerations render the test construction operations more understandable and more conceptually integrated; the empirical tasks render the theoretical considerations more germane and concrete. To this extent, at the beginning of each chapter in part B we summarize the important theoretical considerations for the empirical topics covered. Also, although the two sections of the text have a rough correspondence, we do not intend for this organization and correspondence between the two sections to result in a stilted, mechanical, or even formulaic exploration of the material. Ultimately, we hope that individual readers will find ways of using our book that best suit their particular needs.

For instance, it may be possible to cover two theoretical chapters in class while a certain empirical task is being undertaken out of class. At other times, two empirical tasks flow so naturally one into the other that further theoretical issues might best be held in abeyance while these tasks are undertaken out of class and discussed or reviewed in class. Students may be asked to present their empirical materials, so that other students can learn from each other rather than just from the instructor. This approach has the added benefit of teaching students that different results sometimes are possible when ostensibly using the same procedures, which in turn fosters questioning and discussion about the reasons for the observed outcomes. We have learned that problems of underlying dimensionality, wording of items or instructions, and sampling of subjects need to be revisited repeatedly. We also see the need for researchers who construct their own tests to constantly ask themselves whether their instrument satisfies their concerns for external validity. It is for these reasons that we see the need to make the book much more integrated and intertwined for both theoretical and empirical topics as well as operational and individual research concerns than the table of contents implies.

The foregoing approach presupposes a semester-long, user-friendly course, usually coming no earlier than the second semester of the second year of graduate study, after some prior study of statistics and individual testing and when interest in student-conducted research (for master's, pre-doctoral, or doctoral purposes) has become quite real. Where the quarter system is in effect, the spring (second) of the second year would also seem to be the earliest probable time for these conditions to have been met. We also intend to cater our book to the independent researcher, whose course-work has ended years ago. Such a reader should also be able to use this text on his or her own, perhaps doing so with only minor refresher reading of textbooks from previous courses or some of the recommended texts we list in appendix A.

In part A, the chapters move from general to specific issues concerning the design, development, and implementation of tests for research purposes. Thus, in chapter A1 we begin by describing the context and history behind the idea of using a test to carry out research. We also provide an introduction to measurement and the functions of numbers in this process, with an emphasis on formal measurement.

In chapter A2, we make a case for the need to have an external criterion to assess the final validity of a test. We will return to validity in the context of an instrument in latter chapters, but we firmly believe that validity ought to be on every researcher's mind as he or she begins to design an instrument.

We discuss test reliability in chapter A3, explaining its relation to test validity. We argue that test reliability is the upper limit of test validity in that, unless one can be sure that an instrument will produce the same results on different applications, one cannot know whether it measures what it purports to measure.

Chapter A4 considers test validity—specifically, criterion validity. We consider the difficulties associated with finding an easily measurable criterion given the complexity of most social phenomena of interest to researchers. We also review approximations to this criterion, such as expert opinion, other related tests, the presence of groups associated with the criterion, using existing measures of aspects of the phenomenon or criterion, and relying on demographic data.

In chapter A5, we discuss the theory behind item analyses that include the following categories: Item Difficulty, Item Reliability, and Item Discriminability. These analysis categories reflect our concern with validity and reliability not only for the entire instrument but rather at the item level.

We close this first section with chapter A6, where we consider objections made to Likert scales and review two additional scales: Thurstone and Guttman. We discuss theoretical issues related to the notion of a scale in general and to the particular attributes of these two scales.

Part B focuses on the empirical and practical aspects of test construction. We begin in chapter B1 by discussing the components that make up a test for research purposes. We emphasize the need to become familiar with the relevant literature before drafting any items. Doing so reduces the chances of wasted efforts rushing into collecting data with instruments lacking in construct and content validity that may be confusing to respondents and, eventually, even to the researcher. In this chapter, we also discuss the wording of items, the choice of responses, and the general layout of the test.

In chapter B2, we describe the steps necessary to derive the first version of the test as well as ways to assess it, including performing a dry run with potential respondents. The next step in developing a test for research purposes is to focus on the instrument. Therefore, chapter B3 details the steps in which to carry out item analyses for the first version of the test, followed by a subsequent evaluation of the second version of the test in chapter B4. In this second trial, the criterion validity of the test is highlighted in determining its soundness.

In the last two chapters, we discuss what else to consider once the test's validity and reliability have reached satisfactory levels. Chapter B5 contains a discussion of semiformal measurement as pertaining to tests either directly or indirectly. Though we favor an approach to research that is empirical, objective, and as free as possible of bias, error, or confusing explanations, we realize that the world is not always an ideal setting for inquiry. Therefore, in chapter B5 we introduce content analysis as an approach to research that involves the researcher either in quantifying existing data or in quantifying data she or he generates.

Finally, with chapter B6, we close the empirical section of the book by suggesting that, once a particular test's criterion validity has been satisfactorily demonstrated through repeated uses, the next level of test development is the consideration of additional evaluations for the test's construct and internal validity. We also offer words of advice for researchers wishing to develop their tests for operational purposes, which, as we have explained, implies a different set of considerations.

We chose to illustrate notions related to testing and procedures necessary for test development with several examples of test items at various stages of development. These examples typify the work that students in our courses turn in. To aid the reader in remembering the various scales and particular projects on which these are loosely based, we have used pseudonyms for both our students and their tests. In no way, however, do we intend these examples to be seen as ideal items or instruments. Instead, we want to provide the reader with tangible examples for reference in discussing the material. We hope that, by providing the reader with work representing authentic efforts by student-researchers, he or she will not only have a better grasp of the process and skills involved but also be persuaded of the potential that developing tests for research purposes has in the preparation of researchers.

It is in this same spirit that we include a sample set of items and scores in appendix B to provide practice material for the various procedures. Such a sample set may be attractive to those readers for whom the option of developing their own instrument is not possible. The reader may also choose to use this data set to compare the results obtained after analyzing his or her own test scores.

At various points throughout the book, we offer practical rules of thumb that suggest a quick answer to common questions. For instance, we mention using such a rule to decide when to consider developing a better instrument if many items are left unanswered. Our motivation in including these bits of practical information is in keeping with the practical focus of the book. We have learned that inexperienced researchers are likely to spend much time and effort considering all the possible consequences of relatively minor decisions. Conversely, experience has taught us to anticipate crucial points in the process of test design, evaluation, and development that inexperienced researchers are likely not to notice until too late. So, with an eye to practicality and content that is appropriate for the intended audience of this book, we do not include elaborate theoretical derivations for the advice. Neither do we provide copious empirical, statistically significant evidence supporting their use. Rather, we appeal to common sense and pragmatism when suggesting criteria, decision thresholds, or easy-to-remember rules for particular steps along the way. As we have stated, our goal is to provide student-researchers or beginning researchers with an accessible means to embark on quantitative research.

Prior Assumptions of This Text

What follows is a list of what we consider are basic prerequisites to successfully carry out the procedures described in this book. This list is neither exhaustive nor strict, however. We provide it as a way for readers to assess their own level of readiness to successfully develop a test for research purposes in the manner we propose. For readers not meeting one or several of the assumptions listed, the list may be used as a guide for securing the expertise necessary to complete specific components of the approach we describe. Better yet, the list may suggest topics or skills they might consider gaining greater proficiency in.

1. *The reader is familiar with and has easy access to a recognized text on the use and evaluation of commercially available tests and other quantitative instruments.* We recognize the unique circumstances that surround every research project, circumstances that often require unique treatment. At the same time, much effort and resources have been devoted to developing tests for a host of research applications. There is no reason to reinvent the wheel, especially when, as we will see, much information exists about the performance of commercially available tests.

2. *The reader has studied descriptive and inferential statistics at least through the level of multiple correlation.* No attempt will be made in this text to define or discuss such elementary statistical terms and techniques as *means, standard deviations, variances, degrees of freedom, tests of statistical significance, the normal curve,* or *one-tailed versus two-tailed tests of significance,* for example. These matters are usually covered in the first full year of study of descriptive and inferential statistics. Normally a semester but preferably a full year of such study is a prerequisite for engaging in test construction for research purposes, at least in the manner described in this book.

3. *The reader is able to gather data from at least two equivalent samples of subjects, each consisting of at least twenty individuals (a larger sample is preferable) that are in the* target population *under study in connection with the research being contemplated.* In addition, the reader must be able to locate and test yet a third *contrasting* sample of similar size. The reader must decide whether to select equivalent samples according to the sex, age, ethnicity, religion, health, or socioeconomic status of the subjects or whether to allow all these variables in the sample to vary randomly. Suffice to say that

this contrasting sample should be from a population that, although essentially similar to the target population in almost every important respect, differs from it in at least one crucial aspect. The crucial difference should be chosen with the research literature in mind, such that the third sample's test scores can be expected to be significantly different than those of the target population. We elaborate further on the nature and composition of the contrasting sample in chapters A2 and A4.

4. *The reader has access to and has the training necessary for using a computerized statistical package.* Test construction entails data-processing efforts that are usually considered, in this day and age, to be too complex and time-consuming to engage in without the help of a computer and a program that will generate the statistics that are required even by the most elementary test construction processes. (We have used SPSS in our courses, though the computations needed for the procedures in this book should be available in most statistical packages.) This text will not provide instruction as to how to operate any of the many available computers or install and operate the statistical packages. We have included, however, all the necessary instructions to perform the specific statistical operations in SPSS that we describe in appendix B. Also, many first-year statistics courses often include instruction in the operation of specific statistical packages, and computer centers at many universities can provide the necessary support.

Finally, it should be stressed that we will only focus on *nonphysiological* measures; that is, we will consider tests that measure self-reported attitudes, beliefs, convictions, opinions, and knowledge to the exclusion of other variables. Tests of bodily functioning per se are outside the purview of this text.

PART A

~

THEORETICAL TOPICS

∼

What Are "Tests for Research Purposes"?

Researchers in the social and behavioral sciences, be they students or professionals, are constantly in need of new tests to advance their own short- or long-term research purposes. One of the authors (J.A.F.), as a student, decided to study negative stereotypes that minority children in the United States held about Caucasian, mainstream Americans. This was a rather new topic then, since usually the reverse direction of negative stereotyping had been examined (i.e., mainstream children's negative stereotypes about minorities). To explore his topic, J.A.F. constructed a measure that would enable him to quantify the extent to which minority children accepted or agreed with negative stereotypes about mainstream Americans.

Students in our courses have investigated, among others, the following topics: relationship between religiosity and premarital sex; the role of personality factors in the differential ability of individuals who take care of Alzheimer's patients to resist burnout at their often frustrating and thankless tasks; the contribution of information about the causes of AIDS to the modification of sexual behavior among lower-class minority females; the extent to which study and travel abroad have made Americans more positive toward foreign-language instruction in American high schools; the attitudes of people toward bilingual education in light of their political inclinations. In each case, it was necessary to measure one or more variables that had not been previously studied and, therefore, not specifically measured. Obviously, the soundness of the outcomes of such investigations depends quite substantially on the soundness of the measures that are created by the researchers pursuing them. Quantitative instruments such as questionnaires or scales of one sort or another are the tests that researchers commonly use as measures. Not all social and behavioral research involves the use of tests, of course, but this approach has its advantages, as we will see.

The word *test* is rather old in the English language, one of the few languages that enables its speakers to differentiate between "tests" and "examinations," two closely related concepts. Examinations often focus on cognitive and behavioral skills (e.g., Graduate Record Examination, Scholastic Aptitude Test), in which responses are typically considered either right or wrong. Examinations also measure physical characteristics (e.g., hearing examinations, driving examinations) in which clearly there is not only more and less, but better and worse. Tests, in contrast, also refer to attitudinal and other self-reported characteristics for which individual comparisons of degree for each variable are of interest to the researcher; these kinds of tests typically do not have either right/wrong or physical dimensions.

The term *test* itself goes back to alchemy. In attempting to determine the gold content of any substance or compound, alchemists would place scraps of the material being studied into a small, inert earthen cup and expose the cup and its contents to ever-higher temperatures. This cup was known as the "test," and our expression "to stand the test" is derived from that exposure to high temperature that alchemists used to boil off baser metals. Their hope was that this procedure would yield noble metals. We have seen a similar disposition with researchers as they begin compiling data, particularly when the instruments used emerged more from intuition and hope than from a disciplined approach.

Some of the principles that the alchemists used for testing metals also apply to tests for research purposes today, and it is these similarities that have prompted the extension of the term from its original to newer contexts. Just as the alchemists placed within their tests only a small sample of the entire metallic material that interested them, so we include on our tests only a sample of probes (or items) that deal with the attitudes, opinions, and beliefs that we are interested in. Like the alchemists of old, we do not consider the tests to cause that which is of interest to us; the tests are merely inert vehicles that enable us to separate these characteristics for attention in order to measure them. Of course, the matters that interest us are constructs abstracted from the totality of characteristics that humans present (e.g., attitudes, intelligence, personality), rather than concrete physical entities. We rely on tests for this purpose, so that we can differentiate between individuals in terms of who has more and who has less of these characteristics. Tests are measuring devices. *Introduction to Test Construction in the Social and Behavioral Sciences* deals with the formal principles for constructing the measuring devices that social and behavioral scientists so commonly need to advance their research.

What Is Formal Measurement?

Both *formal* and *measurement* are terms that require some definition. Measurement involves the assignment of numbers to phenomena in such a way that some property of the numbers also pertains to some property of the phenomena. The more that this is so, the better. It could be said that the key to quantitative research is to come up with mathematical models of the real world that not only describe phenomena but actually allow us to predict them.

Properties of numbers exist at various levels of sophistication. At the simplest level numbers merely identify; that is, they distinguish one item from another. Social Security numbers, license plate numbers, on the one hand, and numbered demographic categories (e.g., 1 = Protestant, 2 = Catholic, 3 = Jew; or 1 = male, 2 = female), on the other, illustrate the use of numbers merely to differentiate rather than to quantify. This level of measurement is referred to as *nominal*, because the numbers merely designate the individuals to which they are assigned and carry no implications as to more or less, better or worse, or even first or last. Although tests do not make very much use of nominal measurement, we will note occasions when nominal measurement may be quite useful in test validation efforts.

A more advanced use of numbers is to indicate "more and less" along some continuum. This can be done without indicating how much more or how much less; that is, no explicit metric needs to be involved. Thus, individuals can be ordered by height, without knowing how tall anyone is. Similarly, individuals can be ordered by how many tasks they have completed, without knowing how difficult the tasks are or whether the differences in their difficulties are such that each is equally distant in difficulty from the one that comes before and the one that comes after it. Much measurement in the social and behavioral sciences is actually of this type: *ordinal* measurement. Still more refined levels of measurement are possible, which perhaps explains why ordinal measurement as such receives relatively little mention in the research literature.

Yet a more useful use of numbers can be found at the *interval* level of measurement. At this level, it is possible to develop measurement units that are separated by regular intervals. These intervals, in turn, correspond to equivalent variations for the variable in question. Examples include IQ scores and Mental Age scores as well as some attitude scale scores, where we can speak of equally appearing score intervals. We should note that, in none of these cases, however, is there a real zero. We do not know what an IQ of zero is, but we do know that the difference between a Mental Age of 6.5 and 7.5 is the same (in units of mental age) as the difference between a Mental Age of 12.5 and 13.5.

The highest level of measurement is the *ratio* level. An example of this level is the use of percentile scores, where the units represent the proportion of people who score below any given score. For percentiles, there is a true zero. As with interval measurement, just as many people score between the twenty-fifth and the thirty-fifth percentile as between the eightieth and the ninetieth percentile (even though the score ranges may be quite different between these two separate percentile intervals), because percentiles are equal units of people. When larger samples are available, individual scores are commonly and meaningfully converted or transformed to percentiles, not only because percentiles have a real zero but also because they contextualize scores. If we know that a given score is only very rarely exceeded (e.g., that "only 2 percent of all individuals score higher than that"), this adds meaning to the score in terms of our total experience with human behavior.

Many operational test scores are converted or reported as transformed scores. However, in constructing tests for research purposes, such transformations are rarely used because the samples are too small and the dimensions studied are not yet well enough understood to gain much from such contextualization. Thus, for research purposes we commonly construct measures that are really only at the ordinal level (i.e., they lack equal units along some metric). If we commonly stretch a point, and pretend that they are more than that, it is because we know that if our samples were sufficiently larger, we could transform them into percentiles or standard scores (i.e., scores expressed as deviations from the means of the distributions in which they occurred). That is exactly what is frequently done with very useful tests for research purposes. When they become operationalized, they yield converted scores that are at the ratio level of measurement.

Formal measurement introduces considerations beyond the nature of the metric by requiring that numbers be consistently assigned to phenomena in accord with certain properties of numbers per se. Formal measurement also requires that this assignment be performed in such a fashion that *the measurer is maximally separated from the measurement*. Private or intuitive knowledge of the measurer (the researcher) should not figure in the measurement process. Researcher characteristics or test situation variables that might influence the measurements assigned to individuals by the test must be minimized, excluded, or randomized out.

In contrast to formal measurement, other research traditions focus on the notion that *measurement is indivisible from and nonexistent other than via the measurer* (ethnography, ratings by observers, interview methods, and most projective methods). These approaches to research differ from formal measurement in the extent to which they separate the measurer from the measured. We should note, however, that the difference may not be as great regarding the use of numbers to describe and analyze phenomena. Quantitative analysis is possible and sometimes a desirable option in studies in which the researcher is part of the phenomenon in question. The use of multiple readers in content analysis of interviews and the use of multiple raters for the observation of human interaction constitute frequent attempts to occupy a middle ground between the extremes of formal measurement, on the one hand, and ethnography by a single researcher, on the other hand.

Research traditions and their methodological histories often contain their own justification and tend to carve territories and constituencies along ideological rather than practical lines. Still, there are practical advantages and disadvantages associated with each research tradition. As we will see in subsequent chapters, formal measurement offers certain correctives and benefits that are lacking in other research methods that do not include tests. Since this can be said of each of the other methods as well, the sophisticated researcher has no alternative but to master and utilize them all, sometimes in tandem one with the other, each to its own best advantage and as separate and independent from the other as possible. Such separation and independence are important, because neither the subjects nor the researchers must be influenced in ways that pertain to the findings of method B by the very fact of having previously experienced method A.

For instance, it is not only possible but rather likely for subjects to search for socially desirable (i.e., "right") answers in a test after answering a series of interview questions as part of the same investigation. The reverse may also be true, in which both the interpretation of and answers given to interview questions are in turn influenced by the subjects' reading a hidden agenda in a test they completed before the interview. The obvious solution to this form of cross-method contamination is to rely on two separate yet equivalent samples. This is not always possible, however, particularly for researchers with limited resources and time. A more promising approach is to build preventive measures against social-desirability artifacts in the wording of test items and interview questions from the start. In any case, the goal is for the two research methodologies to complement each other and offer possible sources of triangulation for the findings in a pragmatic spirit.

What, then, are the particular advantages of formal measurement for research purposes? Keeping in mind that formal measurement maximally distinguishes between the measurer and the measured, the first advantage is the attainment of greater precision in answering those research questions that recognize degrees of the phenomena being investigated. Such recognition is rendered more precise by formal measurements that yield either interval or ratio scores.

Another particular advantage of formal measurement is that it provides a way to estimate the probability that any finding may be no more than a chance or random sample occurrence out of a universe of data from which quite different results would be concluded than those that the sample findings imply. Researchers are often (even usually) quite convinced of the reasonableness of their findings. The findings often make sense and agree with the feel of reality that every researcher develops accompanying a topic to which he or she has devoted a great deal of thought, time, effort, and resources. However, such convictions may be far from objective or self-critical, and even findings that make sense should be required to answer the Doubting Thomas who asks, "What is the likelihood of obtaining these results purely by chance when sampling from a universe in which what you found is not possible?" This is often an annoying or even threatening question to cope with, because the answer to it may require us to redo our work and to improve upon it. Nevertheless, it is a question that ought to be considered throughout any serious inquiry, regardless of method. Using tests for research purposes both brings this question to the forefront and provides definite answers to it. Formal measurements enable researchers to evaluate the validity and reliability of the results. (We will discuss validity and reliability at greater length in subsequent chapters.)

Finally, another particular advantage of tests for research purposes is that they also provide an answer to another difficult and possible upsetting question: "To what extent have I answered my research question by the methods that I have employed?" As stated in the introduction, the approach we propose attempts to account for a maximum variance associated with measurable aspects of a phenomenon or phenomena. Sometimes results can look very favorable to a researcher, and they can even be results that could not frequently have come about by chance sampling factors alone, and yet they can be results that still essentially leave the basic, underlying research question either essentially unanswered or substantially so. Many other methods do not build in this particular Doubting Thomas, and it is to the credit of tests for research purposes that they do not let the researcher off the hook quite so readily.

In short, tests for research purposes regularly produce results of a kind that enable the investigator to be more self-critical than self-congratulatory. Self-criticism is a valuable characteristic for any researcher to cultivate, because it is far better to criticize one's work by one's self, before findings are published or communicated to others, than to be publicly criticized by others after "the fat is in the fire."

~

The End Goal as a First Consideration

We will discuss validity at some length later on, but before we do that, we must say a few words about it at this point. *Validity is the ultimate goal of all test construction for research purposes*. To the degree to which any instrument really measures what it intends to measure, rather than something else, our first consideration in test construction ought to be validity. If we cannot be sure that our bathroom scale measures weight, then how can we use its readings to regulate our diet? If we cannot be sure that the SAT measures basic academic ability, then how can we rely on it to make admissions decisions that result in some applicants being admitted and others being rejected? Clearly, validity is "what it's all about." Research that depends on or uses test results necessarily stands or falls on the validity of the measures contained in these tests.

Test validity may be of two kinds: internal and external. Evaluations of a test's internal validity may consist simply of an analysis of its appearance (i.e., face validity) or be based on the opinion of experts regarding the extent to which a test covers a particular subject area or content (i.e., content validity). Also, it is possible to obtain a preliminary assessment of a test's internal validity by considering the extent to which the test items reflect constructs reported in the research literature (i.e., construct validity). However, a definite evaluation of a test's construct validity must be empirically based.

External validity may consist of a criterion (i.e., criterion validity) or some other outcome that may be predicted (i.e., predictive validity). The external validity of a new test may also be assessed by comparing the test's scores with those of well-established and widely used measures of constructs that are either the same or theoretically related. Construct validity evaluations must include both constructs that are theoretically associated with the construct in question and those that are not. A related evaluation of test validity consists of comparing the scores of a new test with those of well-established, related measures obtained concurrently (i.e., concurrent validity). (See the reference to Patten among the recommended readings in appendix A for a thorough and practical explanation of validity in its various forms as well as its relationship with reliability.)

To demonstrate the validity of an instrument, a researcher must do more than point to characteristics of the instrument itself. It is not enough to say that "it looks right," even if those doing the looking are all well informed and entirely in agreement about what the makeup of the instrument should be. As we will discuss later, in fact it may be desirable for an instrument not to be transparent about its intended purpose. Beyond its appearance or face validity, one may evaluate the validity of an instrument by looking at its content validity. Such an approach is an improvement on basing the evaluation on appearances alone, particularly if the instrument measures an established and clearly defined construct, and those evaluating the instruments are experts in the field.

For new instruments, however, unlike a recipe, the proof of the pudding is not determined by its ingredients but *on its ability to accomplish what one should be able to do with it* if it were indeed valid. This may sound a little like putting the cart before the horse, but so be it. One cannot determine validity before knowing (1) what an instrument should be able to do in pragmatic terms and (2) how one will be able to recognize, in the world of behaviors that are external to the test, whether indeed it is able to do those things. If there is absolutely no way to demonstrate, in a consensual fashion and in accord with the accepted cannons of publicly verifiable science, that an instrument is measuring what it claims to be measuring, then it has no place in scientific discourse, regardless of its place in the realms of philosophy, poetry, politics, or some other field.

So how can a budding researcher be sure that a newly drafted instrument is valid before investing much effort and resources on finding out whether the test indeed does what the researcher intended? An essential first step is to familiarize oneself with the research literature before writing any test items at all. The review of the literature ought to include both theoretical and methodological considerations. On the one hand, becoming familiar with pertinent theory goes a long way toward defining constructs associated with variables of interest. On the other, learning about proven research designs and instruments in preparation to developing one's own instrument could potentially save time and effort while contributing to the internal validity of the constructs included in the test. It is in this sense that we mean that validity ought to be foremost in researchers' minds, even if it is not possible to assess at the offset the extent to which an instrument performs in the desired manner. By being mindful of validity that is internal to the instrument from the start and paying particular attention to the validity of the constructs included, researchers can hope for greater external validity. In our view, the latter is the mark of a sound test for research purposes.

Validity indicators may be direct or indirect. For instance, when a person uses a bathroom scale and observes a reading of 195 pounds, this figure must correspond to the equivalent number of pound weights in the Bureau of Standard Weights and Measures in Washington, D.C. However, if that person's blood pressure is 140 over 75, these figures pertain to the height of standard columns of mercury that are related to blood pressure by dint of a century's worth of research on instruments of a particular construction. It is because of this prolonged research, which unquestionably relates the columns of mercury to the strength with which blood is pumped out of and back into the heart, that we are satisfied today that they reflect blood pressure and not temperature or other bodily considerations. Were there no such extensive body of research to clinch the claim that these columns of mercury do indeed measure blood pressure, we would be poorly served to put our trust in them, no matter how sophisticated they might appear to be. Thus, the claim of a measure to validity does not depend (at least not in formal measurement) on whether it looks good to the measurer or the measured, whether it contains all the necessary elements, or whether it is constructed in the way the measurer intended it, much less on whether it yields consistent results.

All the foregoing indicators may or may not be desirable characteristics in their own right. As it happens, we do not always want to have instruments that are transparent to our subjects. Due to natural tendencies in people to be perceived in ways that are socially desirable, we do not always want our subjects to be able to tell whether the instrument looks like it is measuring this or that behavioral dimension. Similarly, demonstrating that an instrument is constructed in the very way that the measurer originally conceptualized or designed it is unimportant. It is the design per se that needs to be validated. As is especially the case with beginning qualitative researchers, novice test-constructing investigators often "feel" or intuitively "know" that they are right, that their theories are right, and, therefore, that their instruments are appropriate. But conviction is not evidence, and self-conviction tends toward self-congratulation and self-delusion.

Construct validity, or the relationship between a particular measure and a large number of other measures, is not really a very satisfactory claim to validity, either. It is an argument, a complex web, a house of cards made up of instruments that lean precariously on each other without any one of them relating to the outside world in any concrete terms. Such claims to validity are ultimately more confusing than amusing, even insofar as their own internal frames of reference are concerned.

Finally, consistent results, although of utmost importance, cannot be confused with validity. The results may be very consistent trial after trial if one were to use a bathroom scale to measure one's intelligence. Yet, these measurements do not pertain to one's mental capacity in the slightest, regardless of how consistent they may be. We will discuss reliability in detail in the next chapter. For now, suffice to say that it is easy to become lulled by a test's consistent scores into assuming that such consistency answers best the question of whether the test does what one set to do from the beginning.

Tests for research purposes must have external validity, at least at the outset. Their internal validity may be quite gratifying, whether it be of the face validity, content validity, or construct validity variety, but no amount of internal validity can substitute entirely for external validity. Unfortunately, however, behavioral research has been better at making validity claims based on internal validity grounds than on demonstrating validity on external or criterion validity grounds. As a result, the appreciable test-building sophistication that has been attained based on factorial evidence and construct validity has seldom been translated into better external validity evidence insofar as correspondence to the real world is concerned.

The importance of considering external validity from the outset of test construction should be especially pertinent to beginning researchers and students. Most procedures intended to boost construct validity require extensive time, resources, and expertise levels beyond those typically available to most readers. *How will the external validity of my new instrument be demonstrated?* This is the ultimate, bottom-line question in test construction for research purposes, a question that researchers would do well to grapple with sooner rather than later. Without a satisfactory answer to this question, the value of any newly constructed instrument remains unconfirmed, and any findings derived from its use easily and undeniably questionable.

Researchers, particularly student researchers, can, should, and do utilize various and, indeed, quite diverse external realities to buttress their claims to external validity for the instruments that they must construct in order to proceed with their research. Some of these include student achievement, divorce rates, incidence of diseases, accident rates, and election results, among others. What these external realities all have in common is that the researcher taps or samples them but does not create them. They have an existence of their own, independent of the researcher's activity. So, what is the researcher's task in demonstrating a test's validity? Simple, yet not always propitious: To relate the test scores of a sample of subjects to the varied performance of the same sample on the selected aspect of external reality.

A correlation coefficient[1] (r) represents an estimate of the relation of two variables such as a test score and an adequate measure of the external reality aspect of choice. Thus, a researcher's claim to validity will depend on whether this correlation coefficient is high enough to substantiate such a claim in the eyes of the research community. How high is "high"—like how far is "up"—depends on one's location at a particular time. In advanced fields with deep research traditions and histories, correlation coefficients[2] above 0.80 are common, so that a result of 0.75 on a student-made instrument is not really something to write home about. On the other hand, in novel and largely unresearched fields, coefficients of 0.75 could certainly be considered encouraging, if not actually quite high. If, as often happens, the correlation coefficient is low, then it is best to know about it as early as possible. Validity can be an elusive, often missing, yet crucial link in research requiring formal measurement. Rather than ignoring early indications of weak external validity, which obviously will not change the sad state of research affairs that may exist, knowing about weak external validity early on often enables us to do something constructive about it. For instance, we may still be able to revise our instruments before investing time and resources (not to mention pride and reputation) on gathering data that are inextricably flawed.

We believe that external validity is a matter of very considerable importance in the total research enterprise, and we will return to it in chapters A4 and A5, as well as in chapter B4. It is a topic that neither can nor should be avoided. We are fortunate, in fact, that formal measurement is a method that does not allow us to escape a constant concern for formal, external validity and that urges us to address it, to improve on it, or, at worst, to acknowledge and make public our deficiencies about it.

Notes

1. Unless we state otherwise, whenever we use the term *correlation*, the reader can assume this is a Pearson product moment or "Pearsonian" correlation.

2. We will follow convention and refrain from using a + sign with correlation coefficients (0.80 vs. +0.80) since all correlation coefficients are positive unless otherwise noted.

~

Instrument Reliability

Reliability is the instrument characteristic that pertains to score constancy or stability from time 1 to time 2, assuming no change in the basic phenomenon being measured. If one gets on the bathroom scale and it shows a weight of 170 pounds, and then one gets off and gets back on a moment later and the scale now shows a weight of 175 pounds, that variation is a reflection of the scale's (un)reliability. What could cause a variation from time 1 to time 2 like that, given that one's weight really could not have changed in the interim? This possible discrepancy reflects a problem that affects all human measurements—namely, that they are not perfectly stable even when the phenomena they pertain to cannot be assumed to have changed. This wobbling is referred to as *error variance*, and it can be caused, in this example, by imperfections in the scale such that if one does not stand exactly on the same spot each time, it will report a slightly different weight. Another source of error might be one's precision in aligning the scale's tick marks with the pointer.

Error Variance and Reliability: Yin and Yang

What might be the cause(s) of error variance in the behavioral and social science measurement fold? One reason for the instability of measures in this area is that subjects sometimes misread or differently interpret the questions that our instruments ask. Sometimes subjects are less attentive than at other times. Sometimes our wording is not clear. Sometimes our subjects are tired, worried, distracted, or simply in a hurry to get finished so that they can go on and do other things. All circumstances that we are not interested in produce instability (or error variance) accompanying the score variance, which we are interested in.

Error variance is simply the reciprocal of reliability. The more error variance, the less reliability, and the more reliability, the less error variance. Every measure we obtain is composed of some of both, and we have no way of really doing away with error variance entirely at any particular time. It is not possible to eliminate error variance for any particular measurement, if only because *we can only safely estimate the degree of error variance in the end.* For instance, we may only assess error variance after noting the discrepancies between repeated measurements of the same unchanged individual on the same instrument.

Although eliminating error variance is impossible, there are various ways of attempting to minimize it by increasing instrument reliability. Of course, extraneous factors influencing test performance should be minimized (noise; poor lighting; fatigue; noxious stimulants such as pain, anxiety, distraction, etc.). Decreasing the speededness of our measures also increases reliability; by allowing all subjects ample time to finish their work, their performance will be less influenced by factors such as stress or distractions. But we are particularly concerned here with instrument characteristics per se that contribute to reliability. All other things being equal, a longer test (i.e., a test with more items) is more reliable than a shorter test, since the more items there are, the less some instability on a particular item or subset of items will destabilize the total score. Furthermore, the more homogeneous a test is (i.e., the more all of its items measure the same, single underlying dimension, rather than a conglomeration of somewhat related and somewhat unrelated subdimensions), the more reliable it will be. Thus, a test of weight alone will be more reliable than a simultaneous test of height and weight all rolled into one. (Since each subdimension contributes independently to the error variance for the grand total, both subdimensions result in more total error variance than would be the case with only one dimension.)

In short, tests for research purposes should be as long and as homogeneous as the traffic will bear. Moreover, if the phenomena we are interested in are multifaceted, then each facet should be measured with a maximally reliable scale of its own (i.e., yielding its own total score).

Ways of Determining Reliability

There are basically three ways in which to determine instrument reliability: (1) by administering the same instrument again to the same subjects, doing this soon enough that the subjects cannot be argued to have changed in the interim (i.e., test–retest reliability); (2) by administering a different but equivalent test to the same subjects after some similarly brief interlude (i.e., alternate-forms reliability); and (3) by estimating the total instrument reliability from comparing the results obtained from two different halves of the same test (i.e., split-half reliability).

Each approach has assets and debits. In test–retest reliability, one correlates the subjects' scores on the first administration of the test with their scores on the second administration. This is a time-consuming and expensive procedure; tests cost money, and the time of subjects or patients, not to mention the time of investigators, is also an expensive commodity. In addition, the conditions and the circumstances of the subjects and of the two administrations per se are usually not exactly the same on two occasions. Thus, test–retest reliability is reduced by time-related error variance. This is also the case, of course, with alternate-form reliability. With some tests, the scores change due to the practice involved in taking each test. This, however, is mostly true of tests that measure skills and abilities rather than attitudes. Moreover, the two forms of the instrument cannot really be absolutely equated, so that item-related error variance creeps in when error variance is estimated by this method.

Because of the foregoing difficulties with both test–retest and alternate-forms reliability, most investigators prefer split-half reliabilities that neither require two administrations nor two instruments for their determination. In this approach, both instrument-related error variance and time-related error variance are either minimized or eliminated (and, not incidentally, the coefficient obtained is usually higher than it would be under the two first-mentioned circumstances and their attendant techniques), because there is really only one instrument—although it is being split into two—and only one occasion.

Two different split-half correlations are frequently employed to determine split-half reliability, and the correct one to use depends on the nature of the items constituting the instrument whose reliability is being investigated. If the items are dichotomous (e.g., true/false, agree/disagree, accept/reject), then the proper correlation to use is the Kuder-Richardson (usually denoted KR 20). If the items are more continuous in nature (e.g., multiple choice), then Cronbach's alpha is the proper correlation to use. Each of these correlations yields *the mean of all possible split-halves* and therefore is much to be preferred over taking some particular split half (e.g., even items vs. odd items) as the basis of determining split-half reliability. Any particular split half may, accidentally, be quite a risky overestimate or underestimate of the instrument as a whole and should be trusted only with considerable reluctance.

Of course, it is possible to randomly assign all test items into two groups and obtain a correlation score of the two. Under these circumstances, besides assuming the responsibility of choosing a particularly fortunate or unfortunate split half, one must use the Spearman-Brown correction. The value obtained from correlating any two particular split halves must be corrected because the scores being correlated are on two mini-instruments, each of which is only half the size of the original instrument. But it is precisely the validity of the original instrument—twice the length of either of the halves—that concerns us. As we have said before, *length itself is a crucial determinant of reliability*. Accordingly, the Spearman-Brown correction permits us to adjust by a factor of two the correlation between the particular halves that have been selected, to compensate for the fact that the split halves are only half the length of the original instrument. No such additional correction factor is necessary when either the Kuder-Richardson or the Cronbach's alpha reliabilities are employed, because the appropriate correction has already been built into them.

Most current statistical packages for the social sciences (e.g., SPSS) provide both Kuder-Richardson and Cronbach's alpha reliability coefficients. Still, it is up to the informed researcher to recognize which one of these two is more appropriate for determining the reliability of his or her instrument, in accord with the item type that predominates therein.

The Correlation Coefficient:
Its Nature, Importance, and Maximization

Since all the measures of reliability—and validity—are expressed by the correlation coefficient (r), it behooves us to pause to examine this useful and seemingly omnipresent type of statistic. The most common correlation coefficient is the one known as the *Pearson product moment correlation coefficient* (named after Karl Pearson, 1854–1936). This correlation varies from +1.00, through zero, to –1.00. The positive values for this coefficient indicate covariation in the same direction (i.e., when the *x* test scores go up, the *y* test scores go up; when the *y* test scores go down, the *x* test scores go down). Negative values indicate that when one variable rises, the other falls. The word *coefficient* means "multiplier." The correlation coefficient informs us of the degree to which completely proportional covariation exists between two sets of scores (i.e., when the covariation of the one is a multiple of one of the covariants of the other). When this type of covariation occurs, then the correlation is +1.00 or –1.00; and when it does not occur, it is some multiple of +1.00 or –1.00 that is less than one.

The full name of the coefficient, Pearson product moment coefficient, gives us a very important understanding of what it represents. Another expression of product moment that we are all acquainted with is the seesaw. Small weights that are far from the fulcrum on one side of the seesaw can balance large weights that are close to the fulcrum on the other side, because the product of the moment (weight times distance) of the one can equal the product of the moment of the other. A baby can balance an elephant, theoretically, if the baby, on one side, is far enough from the fulcrum and the elephant, on the other side, is close enough to the fulcrum. The Pearson product moment correlation expresses the degree to which two sets of scores for the same individuals are similarly dispersed on their respective seesaws around their respective fulcrums. In addition, however, the greater the dispersion of the scores (i.e., the greater the score variance) on each measure, the greater the numerical value of this correlation. Where there is no such dispersion, there can be no correlation between two sets of scores. If everyone gets the same or almost the same score on any test, or on any variable, then that test or variable cannot correlate well with any other test or variable.

We will illustrate this point with an example: We all know that, overall, height correlates well with basketball success. However, if there is no variation in height (i.e., all the players are very tall or all the players are very short), then height ceases to correlate well with basketball success. Other characteristics of the players must then be responsible for any differences that exist in basketball success, such as speed, accuracy, stamina, and motivation, among others. Similarly, all other things being equal, the reliability of an instrument that does not yield much score variance cannot be as great as that of an instrument that does yield considerable score variance. Longer instruments yield more score variance than do shorter ones.

Unspeeded instruments yield more score variance than do speeded ones. Items that yield more varied responses contribute more to total score variance than do items that everyone answers in the same fashion. A test (or an item) that frequently yields no-response answers (or, indeed, answers of any other given response option) will be less reliable for the same reason: it will simply yield less score variance.

A greater diversity of talent in the subject pool will enhance a scale's reliability, and a homogenization of talent will undercut that reliability. Clearly then, some factors influencing reliability are dependent on (1) the instrument's ability to adequately yield or recognize a greater range of talent and (2) the availability of such a range in the samples being studied. Researchers creating research instruments should take pains to build in both types of score variance: internal and external to the instrument per se.

We have one final observation as to the correlation coefficient. We all know that *correlation is not causation*. However, if we are interested in causation (or in its approximation or estimation via prediction), then the correlation coefficient must be squared $(r^2)^1$ to reveal the extent to which (in percentage terms) variation on one variable predicts variation on the other. If high intelligence causes or predicts high scores on the SAT, then the square of the correlation between them is an expression of the extent of causation or prediction that exists between them. In other words, if the reliability of an instrument is 0.90, then 81 percent of its score variance between one administration and another is an expression of true variance in the sample on the variable being measured. The rest (19 percent) of the score variance from one occasion to the next is attributable to error variance (imperfections in the instrument or "static" in the test taker or in the test-taking context).

It is important that we make it clear that, in squaring the correlation coefficient between two test applications, we do not assume the existence of a true score. We simply see this procedure as a useful way to assess the extent to which one score predicts another. That the correlation coefficient can also be easily related to degree of causation or prediction is an extremely important part of its appeal for test constructors. Other statistics are either statistically significant or not, where *significant* usually means no more than a very minor probability of being derived from a universe in which the null hypothesis is proven true. The correlation coefficient can also be interpreted in terms of statistical significance, but it alone answers the question "To what extent has my search been completed; to what extent is the criterion accounted for, explained by or predicted by the predictor?" Or, to put it in practical terms, "To what extent are students' SAT scores accounted for, explained by, or predicted by their intelligence?"

Even a low correlation can be statistically significant given a large enough sample size, but a low correlation essentially tells us that our job of prediction or explanation is a long, long way from having been completed. This is something even more important to know than the likelihood of chance results. And being able to know them both through the correlation coefficient and that statistic alone makes the correlation coefficient an exceedingly important statistic to obtain when constructing tests for research purposes. Since most researchers reading this book are likely to rely on small samples for their investigations, we are less concerned about the likelihood of spuriously statistically significant scores swaying the researchers' interpretations of the findings. On the other hand, we encourage the reader to revisit the question concerning the extent to which the test scores account for the variance on the phenomenon in question.

As we will soon note, the Pearson product moment correlation is not the only correlation coefficient that researchers come across in the construction of tests for research purposes. It is, however, the granddaddy of all correlation coefficients and the one that is best known and best understood. All other correlation coefficients are either estimates of it or are compared with it in any consideration of their respective characteristics, assets, and debits.

The Logical and the Operational Implications of Reliability

When constructing tests for research purposes, reliability is of great interest primarily because it is the upper limit of validity (see chapter A4). *Validity can be no higher than reliability.* Indeed, if we cannot be sure what weight will be reported every time we get on and off a scale in rapid succession, then it is too early to worry about whether the scale is really reporting weight or something else. Conversely, reliability is no guarantee of validity. A scale might be telling us how much the floor below yields to our mass when we think it is actually measuring our weight. Furthermore, even if its readout is completely reliable (dependable, stable), this is no guarantee that it actually measures weight. A panel of judges may agree that the world is flat or that handwriting is indicative of personality (a sign of interrater reliability), but that does not mean that the world really is flat or that handwriting really is indicative of personality. However, if the raters cannot even agree with each other, then there is no point in pondering the validity of their judgments or interpretations.

Another consideration comes to the fore when and if tests that are initially for research purposes go on to also be operational tests—in other words, tests that are used for real decisions concerning the individuals who take them. When that occurs, it is common to have cutoff scores, such that individuals who score below a certain score are not admitted, or are not accepted for treatment, or are fired, or are denied a raise, just as sometimes individuals who are above a certain score are sometimes promoted, rewarded, or given some other sort of special recognition. As we have noted before, the reliability of an instrument takes on a new importance when such cutoffs are used as a basis for differential treatment. The lower the reliability of an instrument, the greater its standard error of measurement and the less certain one can be that an individual's obtained score being close to his or her true score. Tests for research purposes do not need to bear the responsibility of possible errors in decision making vis-à-vis the fate of individuals. Yet, this is no excuse for researchers to discount reliability when designing, testing, and developing tests for research purposes.

For instruments that need to be employed not merely for research purposes, but for purposes of differential treatment of individuals such as acceptance or rejection for membership, hiring or firing, promotion or demotion, admission or nonadmission, all dependent on a test score, the degree of error variance in an instrument becomes quite relevant. Indeed, it is a crucial issue, one that determines the fate of individuals. If individuals were tested infinitely many times, we could determine the standard deviation (of the sampling distribution) of their scores. That standard deviation is referred to as the *standard error of measurement* (i.e., SEm) of these scores.

The SEm can then be utilized to answer questions such as, "What is the probability that a score obtained on any particular occasion is the result of random error factors?" The SEm is a score range such that the probability of an individual's true score, lying within or without various multiples of that range, can be estimated, given the instrument's reliability across many individuals. This probability can guide operational decision makers in arriving at the decisions that administrators, educators, physicians, and others often have to make. An instrument's reliability across many individuals is obviously useful in making decisions with that instrument regarding particular individual tests. However, instruments created solely for research purposes are not to be used for operational purposes. Researchers creating instruments created for research purposes may also make use of this line of reasoning in considering whether the difference between any two statistics (e.g., the mean of group 1 and the mean of group 2) has a particular probability of chance occurrence. This probability estimate is arrived at by examining the aforementioned difference between means in relation to its own standard error of measurement. It should be noted that a difference between means is also a statistic, just as a single score or a single mean is a statistic.

Building better reliability is one of the ways in which investigators try to contribute to ultimate validity. "Good reliability" cannot really be prespecified by way of a uniform range of values that applies equally well to the measurement of all human dimensions, any more than "high" can be given a uniform definition without knowing in advance whether one is referring to the human high-jump, the height of buildings, or the height of airplane flights. All we can say about reliability, therefore, is that it is substantially within the researcher's power to contribute to it, to influence it, and to nurture it, both by instrument design and by sample selection. Accordingly, reliability is a responsibility that the researcher should take seriously because it will affect all of his or her subsequent findings with any instruments the investigator constructs.

Note

1. The reason for using a lower-case r^2 to represent a squared Pearsonian correlation coefficient is to differentiate it from a squared regression coefficient (R^2). Although related, there are important differences between the two statistics.

~

Instrument Validity

In discussing validity, we must reiterate a point made in the introduction: An external criterion must be the ultimate test of validity for a test if we are serious about our ability to explain the phenomena we study. A concern for instrument validity is perhaps the central concern of the entire test construction enterprise. Without adequate assurance as to validity, nothing else matters or really makes much sense. Why should researchers be concerned about their instruments' scores' constancy or stability (i.e., reliability) if they are not even sure that they are measuring whatever they think they are measuring? What consolation is it that their theoretical constructs are complex and elegant and that the tests that they devise faithfully reflect these constructs, if they cannot clearly demonstrate the fidelity, veracity, or the truth value of either that complexity or that fidelity? Nevertheless, the items and overall design of a test *must* originate in sound theory and stand on the shoulders of previous research. An understanding of the theory relevant to the area of interest is essential not only in coming up with a solid test for research purposes but also in interpreting results.

Formal measurement derives from a tradition that seeks more publicly verifiable evidence than the individual researcher's convictions and more convincing empirical evidence than the instrument's fidelity to the theoretical model that inspired the researcher's efforts. It is from this empirical tradition that we see the need to give precedence to criterion validity, or validity that is external to the instrument, when discussing the construction of tests for research purposes. In saying this, we do not mean to discount the need to review the research literature and understand appropriate theories and research in preparation to developing an instrument. On the contrary, the very complexity of most social phenomena requires that researchers become fully familiar with the constructs involved. Only through careful consideration of theory and past research can researchers count on developing tests that have desirable levels of internal validity. Nevertheless, internal validity is but the starting point in the long road leading to a deeper understanding of behavioral phenomena. As such, the ultimate claim to validity must involve some criterion that can be (1) claimed to be the "real thing," the very behavioral phenomenon the researcher has set out to measure or a reasonable substitute thereof, and (2) a demonstration that the test predicts or accounts for that criterion at some level of satisfaction to the scientific community at large.

But if that "real thing" criterion exists and can be independently measured even before and outside the researcher's newly constructed instrument, what then is the justification for constructing the instrument to begin with? Well, often the "real thing" is quite difficult, time-consuming, or expensive to measure. Doing so often requires much expert time and cooperation. Researchers undoubtedly would welcome a test that reasonably approximates measuring the "real thing" and does so more expeditiously, requiring the expenditure of far less time, money, or expert involvement. Such an instrument could be validated against the "real thing" (notwithstanding the cost of doing so); and, if it produces highly correlated results, then the instrument could be used in the future with considerable savings for all concerned. Thus, no matter how subtle and sophisticated the theoretical underpinnings of one's research, there must always be a real criterion, a real use, a real decision, a real task, a real behavior that the test allows us to better do, make, carry out, and understand or explain.

It is the researcher's responsibility not only to be clear and open about the test construction methods used but also to specify and tap or reflect in some fashion the criterion that the newly constructed test is being designed to predict, account for, or explain. There is no new measure that can or should escape or avoid this responsibility. To do so is to indulge in an endless escape from measuring the very reality for which tests for research purposes are ultimately needed and are presumably designed to predict, explain, or account for.

To the rhetorical insistence "No one has ever measured this before, so how can I validate it against the 'real thing' or even against some reflection of the 'real thing'?" the answer must be "What would you or other researchers have used to measure whatever it is that you think your new instrument will measure, *before* yours became available?" Whatever that is—difficult or unsatisfactory though it may be at the moment—that is what your initial criterion should be for your new instrument. Perhaps better criteria will be found in the future, and when that occurs, your test can then be redesigned and revalidated against those better criteria. At any given time, however, there must be at least one criterion that investigators are willing to take as an outside, independent approximation of the "real thing" and to let their work stand or fall by their instrument's success in predicting, accounting for, or explaining that.

The criterion occupies a crucial and also a unique position in the total test construction enterprise. Test constructors can work away at improving their tests. After all, the many ways of maximizing reliability are all under the control or power to influence of test constructors, and reliability is but the ceiling to which we can aspire as far as validity is concerned. Yet, the "real thing," the criterion by which the validity of the test will be ultimately determined, is something that is essentially beyond their ability to influence. It must be captured or approximated as fully as possible, but it is, ultimately, a reality that is substantially if not entirely beyond the test construction process itself. It may require ingenuity to find it and great care, patience, and skill to get it. Yet, it exists somewhere out there, and it is the test constructors' responsibility to locate it, capture it as fully and accurately as possible, and abide by the ensuing results when "it" is used as the reality that one's test results are compared to. It may be up to the investigator to define such an external reality and defend it as a reasonable criterion. Nevertheless, that is what test construction is really about: the researcher's ability to construct an instrument that will come closer than anyone has come before to predicting a reality that is independent of and beyond the researcher's ability to create or manipulate.

At this point, a cautionary note is necessary regarding the selection of the external criterion for test validation purposes. First, the process of choosing such a criterion must be based on a clear conceptual framework that emerges from the research literature. Researchers need to ask themselves whether the criterion of their choice is part of the phenomenon that the instrument measures. For instance, if the test for research purposes measures students' study skills, the external criterion cannot be the amount of time that the student devotes each day to studying. However, if after reviewing the literature the researcher finds a direct relation between studying skills and academic achievement, the latter becomes an

obvious external criterion for this particular test. Once the external criterion is chosen, care must be taken to ensure that the statistic used as the
external criterion indeed corresponds to such and not to a related variable. In other words, an appropriate measure for the external criterion in
our example would be the students' grade point average, but not their self-
rated academic skills.

The ability to come up with a measure specific to the external criterion
will vary depending on the extent to which this criterion is part of the research tradition of a given field. In some instances, the best option may be
a proxy. Again, we cannot overemphasize the need to become familiar
with the pertinent theory and research literature; they both ought to inform the decisions associated with this process. Later in this chapter, we
will address the special needs of test construction for research purposes in
areas that may lack readily available measures.

Besides making sure that the external criterion of choice has a well-
documented, direct link with the phenomenon that the test measures, the
external criterion must also have measurable variance against which to
compare the variance of scores from the test itself. To this extent, external criteria for which a dichotomous measure is the only possible (e.g.,
yes/no, present/absent, active/inactive) may not be the best. Finally, the
external criterion that the test predicts must have explanatory value. If for
example, the external criterion predicted by a particular test is whether
test takers are male or female, the creators of such a test would have a difficult time convincing fellow researchers of the usefulness of this particular instrument.

Does the "Real Thing" Ever Exist in Nature?

If we are building a scale to measure weight, we can compare or calibrate
its results with the results obtained with standard units of weight that are
kept by the Bureau of Weights and Measurements. Although the blood
pressure gauge produces readings consisting of the height of columns of
mercury, those heights have been shown to correlate closely with a variety of accurately defined physiological manifestations. The construct
"blood pressure," in turn, includes all such manifestations together. However, as soon as we leave the reality of the body and other physical phenomena, the question arises whether "real thing" can ever be identified in
a domain other than the test that measures it. It may be rather rare but
not impossible to come across "real thing" in the social and behavioral sci-

ences where constructs are the usual dependent variables of interest. What follows are some examples of ways to assess the criterion validity of a variety of tests of social and individual behavior.

Tests that try to predict the probability of divorce can be validated by comparison to divorce records that are kept in various jurisdictions and available nationwide in large data banks. Comparing entrance and exit polls on the same voters can validate tests that attempt to predict voting behavior. Specifically, results from responses to tests predicting the probability of divorce in four years, for instance, can be compared with the actual four-year divorce rates for an equivalent sample. Tests that are intended to predict purchasing behavior can be confronted with subsequent purchasing behavior records. Age claims, schooling claims and other demographic claims, voter registration claims, housing characteristics claims, income claims, nativity claims, and so forth, can often be validated against local governmental and institutional records.

In the end, it is often painfully clear that the "real thing" is difficult to find and to quantify in most social and behavioral test construction and, therefore, the lion's share of test construction in these areas must be concerned with using reasonable approximations to the "real thing" for validation purposes. These reasonable approximations are of a few recognizable types. Researchers may not be fully satisfied with them, but most researchers will recognize them as the next best thing, to be replaced as soon as a better option becomes available. We will now consider a selection of better options to assess the criterion validity of tests.

Expert Opinion

Often there are specialists who are familiar with the very *subjects* that we are interested in measuring. Indeed, such specialists are the ones most familiar with them concerning the very *behaviors* that we are trying to measure. Doctors, therapists, teachers, parents, and spouses are a few examples of such experts who often have a wealth of expertise and familiarity with the phenomena of interest to researchers. Of course, the opinions or impressions of experts such as doctors and therapists may be too costly, biased, or inconsistent, yet, initially no better criterion may be available.

But even these high-priced specialists may need to be trained and even supervised so that they will keep their records in the detail and in the way that the researcher will find most useful. Similarly, specialists must keep records independently from other specialists so that (1) they do not contaminate each other's ratings and (2) they do not have any knowledge of the researcher's measurements of the same subjects. The choice of experts must depend on the criterion by which the validity of the test will be determined. Thus, if a test aims to measure variables associated with the diagnosis of a particular ailment, medical doctors and not patients ought to be the chosen experts. By contrast, if a test measures variables explaining student attitudes toward teachers, students and not teachers ought to be the experts. It is for these very reasons that the potential exists for considerable savings of effort and resources if a test can be made that will ultimately obviate the need to recruit and train high-priced experts.

In every instance where experts are employed, researchers must contend with some level of disagreement among them. This is often done by determining the mean rating per subject across all raters or across all raters on all occasions. However, even obtaining the experts' mean ratings does not necessarily diminish the nagging uncertainty about whether the raters per se are providing valid data or whether the instruments that are employed to collect their ratings are themselves valid. In general, expert ratings may sometimes serve as the "next best thing to the real thing" to validate a particular test, but they also pose problems of their own. Accordingly, there are other ways to finding approximations of external validity criteria besides asking experts who have known our subjects well and over a considerable length of time.

Previously Well-Validated Tests

A frequently used external criterion for validating a new test for research purposes is the extent of its agreement with an established, well-known, previously published instrument. The latter may or may not measure *exactly* what the new instrument purports to measure, but, as far as previously available tests go, it is the next best thing. Furthermore, such tests typically have a proven record of publications and professional experience that back them up. If the new test for research purposes (1) is cheaper to produce, (2) is less time-consuming to administer, or (3) requires less specialized personnel to administer and score (not to mention if it possesses any *two or more* of the foregoing sterling traits), *and* if it correlates well with the old test, then the new test starts off its career with quite a claim to fame.

Of course, the danger with using old and well-established measures is that of infinite regress in validation via correlation. Tests referring to each other for validation may create an endless hall of mirrors with nothing but yet another test score at the end of the road. Therefore, one must be sure that those prior measures were themselves validated in connection with an appropriate outside criterion rather than yet again with some still earlier test. Somewhere, the claim to validity via correlation with prior measures must touch ground, must come face-to-face with an external behavioral reality per se, rather than merely with yet another test. Tests, even tests for research purposes, are essentially meant to describe, predict, and explain more than just other test scores, and the sooner that reality is faced, the better for both the research enterprise and the ultimate applied enterprise that tests are intended to serve.

Validation via correlation with prior tests rests on even shakier grounds when it is purported that the new test measures something slightly different from what the old test measures. In that case, it is hard to say what magnitude of correlational evidence would really be satisfying. If the correlation between the old test and the new test is high when compared with other similar tests, then that would seem to imply that the new test is not really after anything as different as it claims to be. If, in contrast, the correlation is low, then how can such low correlation be used as evidence of validity? Let us assume that the new test for research purposes purports to measure a certain, somewhat different personality construct and that a previously constructed and validated personality diagnostic test is to be used to buttress the claim to validity for the new measure. If the correlation between the two is medium or low, obviously a plethora of irrelevant measures could be found that would also correlate negligibly with any previously available instrument in the personality domain (reading ability being an obvious one). Even if the correlation between the two measures is neither too high nor too low, it is hard to see why this would be comforting evidence insofar as validity is concerned. A validity correlation of .50 is an admission that half of the covariance remains unexplained, and *that* is not usually taken as an encouraging claim to validity.[1] Thus, while a common approach to assessing the validity of new tests is to obtain their correlation with old, well-established, and already validated tests, this is not always the most effective use of the "next best thing" claim to validating a new test for research purposes.

Differentiating between Consensually Contrasted Groups

Another, sometimes more gratifying route to validate a new test for research purposes is to demonstrate that it can correctly and significantly differentiate between two groups for which researchers (and maybe even lay persons) would easily agree there ought to be differences in test scores.[2] These contrasted groups may be either natural or experimental groups. The former are groups that exist above and beyond the researcher's control or influence and may include, for example, men and women, institutionalized and noninstitutionalized individuals, elementary and high school teachers, or worshipers at Orthodox synagogues and worshipers at Catholic churches. The latter are groups that have been differentially treated specifically for research purposes and in turn may include subjects randomly assigned to eating and those randomly assigned to fasting on the day of test administration, subjects randomly assigned to seeing movie A and those randomly assigned to seeing movie B before testing, or subjects given one set of instructions (e.g., "This is a test of ability and intelligence") and those given a different set (e.g., "There are no right or wrong answers on this test") at the beginning of the test. In either case, whether natural or experimental groups are being compared, the confirmation of the new test's claim to validity rests on a consensual recognition that not only must the two groups score significantly differently, but *the results must turn out in a particular predicted direction*. If the test really measures what it claims to be measuring, we would naturally expect one of the group's scores to be *significantly* different than the other.[3]

Nevertheless, this approach to validating a new test for research purposes also often poses problems that limit any claim to validity on this basis alone. Where the contrasted groups exist in nature, they are often suspected of differing in various ways all of which share responsibility for producing the test results. If this is the case, then it cannot be claimed that the dimension that the test is purportedly measuring is the sole reason for any observed intergroup difference in test scores. Consequently, the test's claim to consensual validity is eroded accordingly.

For instance, we may be interested in validating a new test aimed at finding out about people's attitudes toward government spending on public schools. Our criterial groups may consist of subjects including both Republican and Democrat registered voters. On the one hand, it would be comforting to find out that the scores of Republican registered voters tended to be significantly more fiscally conservative than those of Democrats. On the other, one must realize that Republican and Democrats differ from each other in ways other than their respective position on school spending. The differences in test scores between the two groups may be due to a range of related variables such as income, not to mention contrasted beliefs and values associated with public education and government spending in general. This possibility diminishes the validity of the criterion groups vis-à-vis government spending on public schools.

Even when other predisposing factors are controlled or matched, or even with random assignment to (experimental) subgroup membership, the seemingly confirmatory results of groups differing significantly and in the predicted direction can sometimes still be attributed in part to still other circumstances than the dimension being tested. Even more often, an argument from group differences to individual prediction is a difficult and risky one. Significant difference between contrasted groups on the test for research purposes can exist even when the groups overlap quite substantially. For all of these reasons, a claim to validity via the demonstration of significant directional differences between contrasted groups is no more than a tentative claim. It is usually clear even in terms of the proportion of criterion variance accounted for that this approach is merely the beginning of a quest for determining and assuring validity, rather than its conclusion.[4]

Simple and Unforced Stepwise Regression

Before going any further, we need to explain the nature of the quantitative analysis used to determine the predictive power of either scales or tests or both. When a linear relationship exists between two variables, a linear regression equation can be used to predict the value of the predicted or *dependent variable* (the criterion) from the value (or values) of the predictor(s) or *independent variable(s)* (the total test score or one or more scales or subtest scores). Multiple linear regressions are also possible, when more than one predictor variable is used to predict a single predicted variable.

We have found that one of the sources of confusion for students stems from the less-than-descriptive name that Sir Francis Galton (1822–1911) used to describe this statistical procedure. A cousin of Charles Darwin, Galton studied the relationship between the characteristics of parents and their offspring. He noticed that the height of children born to exceptionally tall or short parents approached the mean height of the population. Galton reported his findings in a paper titled "Regression towards Mediocrity in Hereditary Stature."

Things have changed much since Galton used a regression equation to analyze his data, particularly as far as the skills and time required to perform such analysis. Computers and statistical packages nowadays eliminate the computational demands of multiple-regression analysis, making this powerful procedure accessible to researchers with limited statistical expertise. By executing a small set of actions through a keyboard and mouse, we are now able to compare the predictive power of a number of variables on a criterion, both individually and together, in various combinations. A particularly powerful operation is that of asking the computer to find the best combination of independent variables, one at a time, that accounts for the greatest variance in the dependent variable: a *stepwise regression*. The computer program (e.g., SPSS) first finds the scale or measure that has the highest correlation with the criterion and, consequently, explains most of its variance; this is known as the *zero-order regression*. (Remember? We use r^2 for zero order and R^2 for all others.) Next, the program computes the multiple-linear regressions for a combination of two independent variables from all the remaining variables, selecting the one that yields the highest correlation. The program selects combinations of three, four, and more independent variables in the same manner, stopping only when the multiple linear regression reaches a preset level of minimal statistical significance (usually $p > .15$). Since the computer program tests each combination of independent variables separately, it is not uncommon for variables to appear and disappear from the list of best predictors.

Remember that the computer is looking for the highest R^2 value in each step, as it increases the number of independent variables and, consequently, their overall predictive power. The final combination of independent variables is what, in statistical terms, is considered the "model" that best explains the variance of the dependent variable from the available independent variables. Ideally, at this point the model also accounts for close to 100 percent of the dependent variable's (i.e., the criterion's) variance. However, the test construction world, as the reader will soon realize, is far from ideal, and models with R^2 scores of around 0.5 are not uncommon. Nevertheless, stepwise regressions provide us with a way to evaluate both the total and partial criterial validity of tests and their respective subcomponents.

Incremental Validity

Indeed, the sad fact of a researcher's life is that any single basis for claiming validity for his or her tests for research purposes is likely to be rather discouraging, at least in the initial stages of test construction. Validity is simply the weak point of all our efforts. Thus, it is not at all unusual to piece together a test's incremental validity by combining two or more predictors, to see whether *jointly* they will be any more effective in predicting a criterion than one or another. Allow us to illustrate this point.

If we are willing to accept *significant and directionally prespecified group membership differentiation* as our criterion, then we may be gratified to note that the old test and the new test *together* predict this criterion better than do either one of them alone. Being able to account for a greater proportion of the variance in the external criterion measure is enough reason to rejoice, even if the old test is still a better predictor of the external criterion than our new test. Let us use the work of two former students, Preiser and Martin, to make this distinction clear.

Preiser's original goal was an attempt to construct a gender-sensitive instrument to measure test anxiety, wherein the criterion was ability to differentiate between members of group 1 (lower-class children) and members of group 2 (middle-class children). For this, she used Sarason's "Test Anxiety Scale for Children," which in her analysis was very slightly the better predictor of the two after running a zero-order regression for the statistical model. The addition of Preiser's new "Test Anxiety Survey" boosted the multiple prediction of group membership from $R = 0.82$ to $R = 0.86$. However, when the group membership criterion was changed to gender, the stepwise regression order of entry was reversed. Now, Preiser's test was superior to Sarason's, although Sarason's test boosted the multiple prediction from $R = 0.85$ to $R = 0.90$. Thus, even when the previously available test is the better zero-order predictor of the two, the new test may still boost the combined prediction of the criterion to a higher level than was attainable with the old test alone. This is exactly what is meant by *incremental validity*.

Martin's validity demonstration was also essentially of the incremental type, although in her case the criterion was the GCS Test of Depression and not group membership. Martin used the previously developed Billings and Moos Coping Scale in conjunction with her own new test: the "Medical Coping Index." Although Martin's new test produced a higher zero-order correlation with the GCS score ($R = -0.58$) than the Billings and Moos Coping Scale ($R = -0.51$), the two of them together in a stepwise regression model resulted in a cumulative multiple correlation index of 0.69, using the GCS score as the dependent variable (see

Table A4.1. Validity Analyses for Martin's Medical Coping Index, Version 2 (MCI-2)

A. Correlations

Variables	Pearson Correlation Coefficient	p (one-tailed)
MCI II + Billings and Moos Coping Scale	.218	
MCI II + GCS	.576	<.01
Billings and Moos Coping Scale + GCS	.505	≤.02

B. Regression Analyses

Dependent Variable = GCS Scores
Independent Variable = Billings and Moos Coping Scale, MCI II, age, sex, education, marital status, number of children, months since diagnosis, ethnicity, and religion

Predictor Variable	Cumulative Multiple R	R^2
1. MCI II	.576	.332
2. Billings and Moos Coping Scale	.695	.483

table A4.1). Together, these two tests accounted for almost half of the variance in the criterion; individually, the better of the two tests accounted only for a third of that variance.

Using Demographic Characteristics to Increase Criterial Prediction

Essentially the same logic is involved when demographics (rather than tests) are used as the additional predictors in attempting to predict a validity criterion. Using demographic variables is but another effort to discover ways to account for the variance in the criterion over and above that attributable to either the new or the old tests or to both. As we noted, Martin was lucky enough to have two old tests available, which allowed her to use one of them as the criterion and one as a predictor. But that is an unusual circumstance. We will now discuss possible ways to deal with the lack of tests that may either be used to enhance the incremental validity or as external criteria. Again, we will rely on the work by another student, Adachi, to illustrate these points.

Adachi only had one old test available (PSDI). Hence, he used it as his "next best thing" criterion. His predictors were his new test (Caregiver Questionnaire, Version II) and a number of demographic characteristics of the Alzheimer patients who were his subjects or of their care-

Table A4.2.   Adachi's Multiple Linear Regression of the Criterion Level of Mean Distress (as measured by the PSDI) by the Optimal Model of Predictor Available with Caregiver Questionnaire, Version 2 (CQ-2) Scores

Variable	Multiple R	R^2	Change in R^2	F
Caregiver Questionnaire II	.441	.194	.194	9.115
Time since First Symptoms	.489	.240	.045	2.128
Time since Diagnosis	.540	.292	.052	2.449
Spouse in Day Care	.565	.320	.028	1.308
Caregiver's Employment Status	.599	.359	.040	1.853
Combined Monthly Income	.635	.404	.045	2.087

givers. The best single predictor of the lot was his own CQ II (see table A4.2). Its correlation with the PSDI criterion was $R = 0.441$. However, five different characteristics of his subjects or of their caregivers proved to be useful predictors thereafter, step by step, slowly raising the total final multiple prediction of the dependent variable to $R = 0.635$. This is a particularly interesting result, since without his new test, an array of predictors that included several additional tests plus the same characteristics of the subjects and their caregivers finally yielded a multiple R of only 0.599 (see table A4.3). Thus, Adachi, twice demonstrated the superiority of his instrument. When it was utilized, it came in first, as the strongest predictor; when it was not utilized, the total multiple attained score was lower than when it was utilized (even though two other tests were also employed as independent variables). Furthermore, when the old instruments were included with his CQ II and all the demographics in a single unforced forward selection procedure, his new instrument came in first and pushed the old tests out of the multiple linear regression model.

Table A4.3.   Adachi's Multiple Linear Regression Scores for the Criterion Level of Mean Distress (as measured by the PSDI) by the Optimal Model of Predictor Available without Caregiver Questionnaire, Version 2 (CQ-2)

Variable	Multiple R	R^2	Change in R^2	F to Enter
Caregiver in Private Therapy	.263	.069	.069	2.904
Caregiver Takes Psychiatric Medication	.371	.138	.069	2.898
Preferred Activities Questionnaire	.462	.214	.076	3.194
Instructional Acts of Daily Living Questionnaire	.511	.261	.047	1.998
Monetary Value on Caregiver	.542	.294	.033	1.399
Caregiver in Support Group	.575	.331	.037	1.556
Caregiver's Employment Status	.599	.359	.028	1.189

These demonstrations—whether relying on two groups, two test incremental validity designs like Preiser's, or one group, three (or more) test incremental designs, like Martin's and Adachi's—all point in the same direction. The validity of newly constructed instruments for research purposes may be disappointing. Yet, they may still be better than older, prior instruments when the latter are utilized alone. Furthermore, new tests may add incrementally to the overall prediction of a criterion when they are used in concert with either older tests or demographics that characterize the subjects being studied or both.

In psychology, education, and most other social sciences, demographic predictors are often the beginning of further research. Age and sex, for instance, are experiential clues or indicators that may prompt us to inquire, when and if they do turn out to be significant predictors above and beyond our tests, into those further sociopsychological dimensions that need to be measured. Such measurement is necessary to tap into the particular experiences of either age groups or sex groups or both. These experiences, in turn, can make group membership incrementally predictive of the criteria that are of concern to us.

Some demographic predictors may also point to policies that need to be undertaken to counteract societal biases that we do not want to foster as predictors of our criteria. Whether we utilize demographic predictors or decide to counteract them, we first must learn of their existence as effective predictors of the criteria that we are employing. Furthermore, even if we decide to counteract the predictive effectiveness of such demographics as race by constructing racially fair tests, changing the tests without changing the societal and institutional criteria for success is really of little ultimate benefit to the individuals who are penalized by racism. These are clearly issues that go significantly beyond the purview of this book and into that of operational tests for social policy (for further discussion and guidelines about this topic, see Fishman et al., 1964).

Decisions of this sort typify a researcher's quest for greater criterion validity in developing a test for research purposes. The process consists of simultaneously considering both theory and empirical results, playing them off each other, and adjusting the test accordingly. Stepwise multiple regression analyses allow test constructors to evaluate the contribution of single items and scales to the instrument's criterion validity. The question in the reader's mind probably is which of the two to use. We recommend both. Usually the results of analyses that use scales are more productive because of the obviously greater variance in scales. Furthermore, individual item analyses with small samples such as those we assume the reader would perform usually yield limited results because responses to demographic items tend to be dichotomous (i.e., yes/no). In those occasions in which individual items make substantial contributions to the test's incremental validity, the researcher is well advised to consider developing a scale that contains the constructs behind such an item.

The pursuit of incremental validity is, therefore, as basic a concern to the researcher as is the concern for validity to begin with. Accordingly, the researcher ought to reconsider the internal validity question with which the entire process began and either develop a scale that reflects the newly gained theoretical insight or, if necessary, change the direction of research altogether. Thus, when a fourth student, Weiss, discovered that divorce status was a good incremental predictor while validating her Depression Inventory, she had to consider the possibility of including test items representing a new subdimension: stress-insecurity-anxiety. Subsequently, she had to decide whether to include a scale representing this subdimension in a new version of her instrument.

Notes

1. Validity correlations differ from reliability correlations in that the latter must be squared (to determine the proportion of variance in one measure that is accounted for by variance in another measure), whereas validity coefficients do *not* need to be squared and may be interpreted as proportions.

2. Another name for "consensually contrasted groups" is "known groups." However, we chose the former designation because it emphasizes the consensus about membership criteria in these groups that the public at large or the research community has arrived at.

3. Thus, a one-tailed rather than a two-tailed test of statistical significance is mandatory when using contrasted group membership as the basis of validity claims for tests for research purposes.

4. Since accounting for criterion variance requires a correlation coefficient (rather than a t-test or an F-test), it should be kept in mind that contrasted group membership is a dichotomous variable. The proper coefficient for determining the correlation between a dichotomous variable and a continuous variable (test score) is biserial or point-biserial correlation, depending on whether the dichotomy is taken to be real (biserial) or arbitrary (point-biserial) in nature. At the same time, we realize that most statistical packages only offer a Pearson product moment correlation, which yield underestimates of the actual correlation.

~

Item Analysis

In this chapter, we will begin to take a look at how to address reliability and validity concerns at the item level. So far, we have discussed reliability and validity in more or less abstract terms. Now we will address ways in which these two notions may be used to guide us in deciding which test items to keep, which items to change, and which items to either substitute or abandon altogether. As we have done so far, we will use the work of former students to illustrate most of these procedures.

We have divided this chapter into three large sections: "Item Difficulty," "Item Consistency," and "Item Discriminability." Each one deals with aspects of items that are important in their own right yet connected to each other. As we will see, test items elicit responses that fall along a continuum, either toward or away from a construct, cluster together, or are sufficiently different from each other. However, an assessment of each one of these three dimensions (i.e., item difficulty, item consistency, and item discriminability) of tests alone cannot be sufficient information to decide the fate of individual items. Each dimension can be thought of as a lens that allows us to evaluate individual test items. Simultaneously balancing the difficulty, consistency, and discriminability of items is indeed a delicate and far from formulaic task. Often, the researcher may decide to retain selected less desirable items regardless of their contribution to one dimension, if such items turn out to be highly desirable on the remaining two dimensions. Thus, the final decision about whether to keep, modify, or discard an item ultimately must be based on a holistic evaluation.

In a similar way in which validity is the prime goal of tests for research purposes, *item discriminability is the prime goal in item analyses*. Yet, test validity is not the *only* goal of test design and development; we also need to know what the reliability of an instrument is before we either accept it or reject it. For each item, we also need to know the extent to which it captures the greatest variance possible of scores for a particular sample (item difficulty) and the extent to which it clusters together with the other test items (interitem consistency). Only after we know an item's difficulty and consistency scores can we assign its full weight to an item's discriminability score.

We believe that, despite being the chief goal in the development of individual items, item discriminability ought to be the last dimension to be assessed. Correspondingly, we recommend that item difficulty be the first dimension that is assessed, followed by item consistency and discriminability. We have several reasons for recommending this order of analysis. First, we see the need to determine the level of difficulty for each item in order to avoid spuriously high floor and low ceiling effects in our test. Also, most people tend to be most familiar with the notion of item difficulty, given their own experiences as students. These facts, coupled with the relative ease within which item difficulty is calculated, are behind our recommendation to estimate a difficulty score for each item first. Next, we recommend assessing interitem consistency, because consistency is complementary to item discriminability, the final dimension in our item analyses. All three dimensions are necessary, although they are not equally important.

Item Difficulty

We are all well acquainted, perhaps even overacquainted, with the concept of difficulty as it applies to areas with consensual "right" and "wrong" responses. When a grade-school teacher says that the word *Mississippi* is difficult to spell correctly, she or he means that fewer students get it right in comparison to other words. In fact, the teacher will often say that *Mississippi* poses more difficulty to spell right than *Florida*, with the word *difficulty* standing for the numbers or proportions of pupils getting these two words right. Thus, each word on a spelling test has its own difficulty level, the distribution of all the various difficulty levels of the items constituting the test can be graphed, and an average difficulty can be computed. If this is done, then it can become even clearer whether

Mississippi is more difficult than most of the items (or than the average difficulty of all items) on the test.

How can we transfer the concept of difficulty from the domain of clearly right and wrong answers to the domain of answers that reflect respondent views, preferences, or behavioral self-reporting? This can be done by redefining difficulty as the *degree of criteriality*—that is, how much each of the response options to a particular item contributes to total score. In this way we recognize that "rightness" is not necessarily only a matter of completely right (one point) or completely wrong (no points) but often one of degree as well. A totally right answer on a spelling test can be scored so that it will be worth more (three points) or contribute more to total score than does a partially right answer (two points), a partially right answer can contribute more than a minimally right answer (one point), and a minimally right answer can contribute more than a completely wrong answer (no points). (Obviously, the teacher would have to define what the criteria for each score are.)

It is important to recognize here that *each item contributes to total score, anywhere between greatly to not at all, when it is scored in the criterial direction.* In our example of the spelling test, criterial direction is the same as the direction of "goodness of spelling." Each item's difficulty level can then be expressed as the average criteriality of response that pupils obtain on it. If an item is scored dichotomously (e.g., right/wrong), then *a more difficult item may be viewed as an item that a smaller proportion of student has responded to in the criterial direction than they have to other items.* If an item is scored continuously (e.g., on a 1–4 scale), then *an item with a lower mean response criteriality than another item is the more difficult of the two.*

From this discussion, it is but a short step to realize that items designed with attitudes, preferences, beliefs, and behavioral self-reports in mind can also be scored for criteriality, reflecting the fact that certain responses are credited as contributing more to total score than other responses to these items. Again, items can be scored either dichotomously (e.g., agree/disagree) or continuously (e.g., agree completely, agree more than disagree, disagree more than agree, disagree completely). And just as a teacher does not want to rely on a test such that all students answer its items either completely right or completely wrong (at least when having to assign grades to students with a range of skills), so *the researcher does not want a test such that everyone answers every item in the maximally criterial or anticriterial direction.* Even more so than the teacher, the researcher is engaged in analyzing variance, whether between groups or between measures. The interest of a researcher creating a new test focuses on the distribution of item difficulties and in the average difficulty of items in the test.

The optimal distribution of item difficulties is a bell-shaped or normal distribution, in which the clustering of most item difficulty scores is around the point where most subjects can be expected to score. If most item difficulty scores cluster roughly at or around *that* point, then it will be possible to differentiate better between most research subjects or to conclude with greater confidence that there is no difference between them. Since fewer subjects tend to score at the extremes of behavioral or attitudinal criteriality, it is really not necessary to have very many items at extreme points in the difficulty range. Nevertheless, a good spread of difficulty is highly desirable, so that researchers can be sure that their instruments do not suffer from spuriously high floors or spuriously low ceilings. In other words, our goal as test constructors for research purposes is to design instruments that allow subjects to reveal their entire range of criteriality of response that characterizes them. The best indicator for this objective is a normal distribution of responses by criteriality that is as balanced as possible and that is neither too flat nor bunched up.

Without analyzing them closely for the desirability or goodness of their distributions of criteriality of response (we will do that in chapter B4), let us look at a few distributions that two former students obtained on the first versions of the instruments for research purposes that they were constructing. Perry was constructing a Fear of Cancer Self-Scrutiny (FCSS) test and permitted respondents to reply on a seven-point scale from zero (least) to six (most).[1] Figure A5.1 shows the distribution of the per-item mean Fear of Cancer Self-Scrutiny criteriality of response, as obtained on the first version of her instrument (FCSS I). Except for the bunching of six items with average difficulties falling in the range between 2.1 and 2.3, Perry's items do tend to cluster, primarily in the 3.0 to 3.8 difficulty range.

As figure A5.1 shows, the mean of all mean item difficulties is 3.2, just somewhat below (i.e., somewhat more difficult than) the mathematical midpoint of the seven-point scale that Perry employed. Martin's difficulty distribution on a five-point scale for an instrument measuring subjects' ability to cope with cancer shows the opposite tendency. Here we note a predominance of items in the criterial direction, such that the mean of the distribution of mean item difficulties is 3.55, or about one-half unit above the mathematical midpoint of Perry's scale. This negatively skewed distribution has a long tail consisting of a few items of great difficulty that few

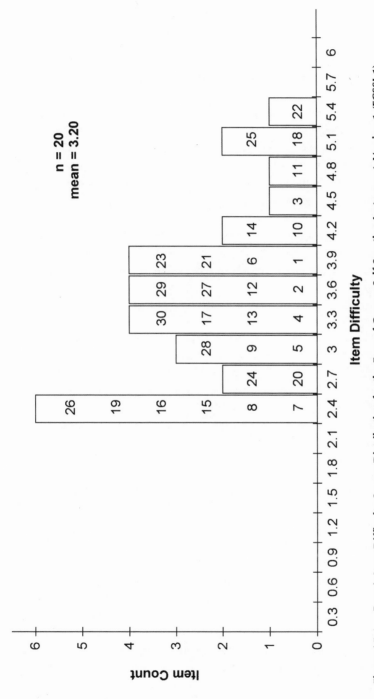

Figure A5.1. Perry's Item Difficulty Scores Distribution for the Fear of Cancer Self-Scrutiny Instrument, Version 1 (FCSSI-1)

Note: Numbers in bars are item numbers.

subjects answered in the criterial direction (see figure A5.2). Both distributions show the bunching effect that would be desired, but both of them require adjustment through deletion or replacement of superfluous items that were either not criterial enough (i.e., too difficult) or overly criterial (i.e., too easy). Tweaking the *distribution* and the mean of mean item difficulties by manipulating specific items is something that test constructors engage in, to improve successive versions of their tests for research purposes. We will describe this process in detail in chapter B4.

So far we have considered only the mean difficulty for each item and discussed the advantages of a test with items clustering around the point where most subjects are likely to score, while simultaneously ensuring that the distribution of item scores captures the range of possible scores for a given sample. Yet, we have not addressed the distribution of scores for individual items. Test constructors do well to wonder about the extent to which they ought to trust each item's mean difficulty score as being representative of the item's difficulty level. In other words, how reliable are the item's mean scores?

Item Reliability (Consistency)

As we have already noted, two of the major instrument characteristics with which all test constructors ought to be concerned are validity and reliability. Each of these instrument characteristics has its corresponding counterpart in item characteristics. Another way of thinking about this is to realize that *the test constructor builds new instruments an item at a time;* therefore, he or she builds instrument reliability and instrument validity an item at a time as well.

How do we build instrument reliability item by item? In chapter A3, we reviewed the characteristics that contribute to instrument reliability. Tests that are longer, rather unidimensional or homogeneous, and less speeded will also be more constant in the scores they yield. The wording of the test items also contributes to the reliability of the instrument. Succinct, unambiguous, and clearly worded items tend to yield more constant responses than long, ambiguous, and obscure items. (See Fowler [1993] for a full discussion about the wording of survey questions; although surveys are not necessarily the same as tests for research purposes, several of Fowler's recommendations apply to tests as well.) Above all, it is important to remember that the basic notion of reliability is *score constancy* between two separate measures on equivalent instruments for equivalent or same circumstances and subjects.

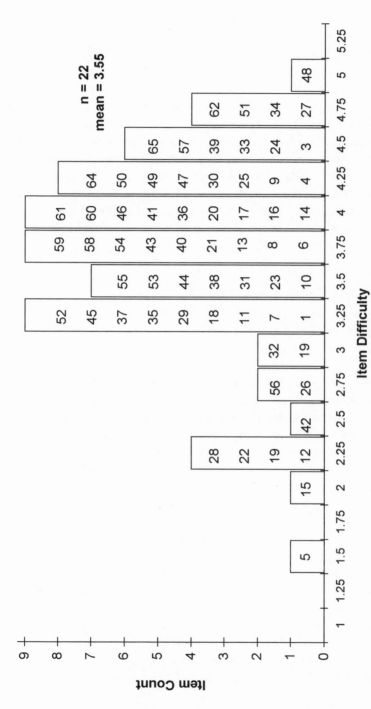

Figure A5.2. Martin's Item Difficulty Scores Distribution for the Medical Coping Instrument, Version 1 (MCI-1)

Note: Numbers in bars are item numbers.

Even if we view the notion of item contribution to instrument reliability at a purely intuitive level, we can grant that the various items of any instrument might well vary in the *degree* to which they contribute to the instrument's reliability. Some items will be more ambiguous than others, more subject to different interpretations on different occasions, some more related to other dimensions than the instrument purports to focus on, and some coming closer to the end of the test when subjects are more tired or more rushed and, therefore, yielding less consistent responses. For these various reasons, the researcher must determine which items are more and which are less desirable insofar as building instrument reliability is concerned. Those items that prove to be the poorer ones on the first version of the instrument can then be replaced when constructing the revised subsequent version. But how are we to determine which ones are the poorer items from a reliability building point of view? What follows is a review of two approaches.

Instrument Reliability If Item Deleted

One approach is simply to recompute the instrument reliability n times, deleting a different item from the instrument each time. Obviously, the deletion of any one item may have only a tiny effect on the reliability of the entire n-item instrument (particularly if $n > 20$), but it will probably have some effect. Items such that their deletion causes the instrument's overall reliability to *rise* are obviously poor items, because the instrument is better off without them. On the other hand, items such that their deletion causes the overall instrument reliability to *fall* are obviously desirable items, since the instrument is worse off without them. Fortunately, it is not necessary to recalculate the reliability of an n-item instrument n times, if one has access to a program such as SPSS. This program and similar others yield this value (expressed as an "instrument alpha-if-item-deleted") simply with a key stroke or a mouse click. (See appendix B.)

The n values resulting from this procedure can then be graphed, and the shape of the entire distribution can be inspected, both as to its contours as well as to where its mean falls. Figure A5.3 is a graph of exactly this kind for the first version of Martin's sixty-four-item Medical Coping Instrument, Version I (MCI-I). Knowing the instrument's alpha value (0.80), it is easy to zero in on the worst items from the point of view of their contribution to this dimension alone. The statistic alpha-if-item-deleted provides an easy guide for item-by-item decision making. However, it is not as informative as one might optimally like item statistics to be. While telling the researcher

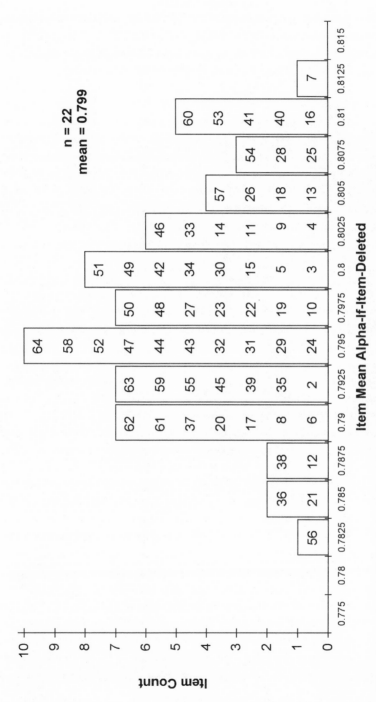

Figure A5.3. Martin's Alpha-If-Item-Deleted Scores for the Medical Coping Instrument, Version 1 (MCI-1)

Note: Numbers in bars are item numbers.

how items are related to the instrument as a whole, it does not tell the researcher how items are related to each other. That is, it does not tell the researcher which items are most consistent with (redundant with) or inconsistent with (negatively related to) which other items.

Interitem Consistency

A second approach to estimating a test's reliability at the item level consists of obtaining an estimate of how well each item "hangs together" with the other test items. We call this estimate *interitem consistency*. The advantage of obtaining an interitem consistency over the alpha-if-item-deleted approach is that it tests the hypothesis that the item in question is similar to the other items, instead of the hypothesis that the instrument's overall reliability is not affected by the specific item.

To determine an item's interitem consistency, it is necessary to obtain its average correlation with every other item in the instrument.[2] However, the well-known Pearson product moment correlation is usually not the optimal correlation to calculate for this purpose. The magnitude of a Pearsonian correlation is greatly diminished by any factors that tend to depress response variance on the dimensions being correlated. Items in tests for research purposes typically are scored either *dichotomously* (i.e., only two kinds of responses are possible) or *continuously* (i.e., typically yield only four or five different answers); in either case, more refined and intermediate responses are not possible. Hence, *the use of the Pearsonian correlation will provide an underestimation of the true interitem correlation present.*

If all items are dichotomous, the most appropriate correlation between them would be the phi correlation or the tetrachoric correlation. If all items are continuous, then the appropriate correlation between them would be the item alpha. Each of the foregoing correlation procedures has a degree of built-in corrections for rough grouping. However, since none of these more appropriate correlation equations are available in most computer statistical packages, frequently no alternative is left but to obtain Pearsonian values and revise them upward. This correction may be done either mentally by adding a constant to all correlation coefficients or computationally by taking advantage of the "Correction for Rough Grouping" function that is provided in many older statistics texts.[3]

Let us use the work of one of our former students, Perry, to illustrate the use of Pearson correlation scores to estimate each item's interitem consistency value. Perry's interitem consistency scores (see figure A5.4) are uncorrected Pearsonians. In chapter A3, we saw that the reliability scores

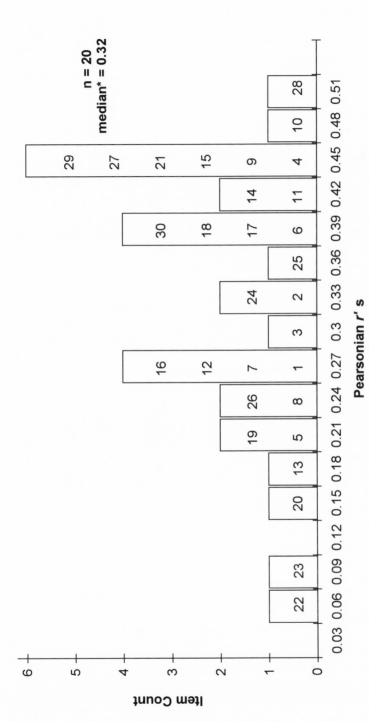

Figure A5.4. Perry's Inter-Item Consistency Scores for the Fear of Cancer Self-Screening Instrument, Version 1 (FCSSI-1)

Note: Numbers in bars are item numbers.

*The large numbers of items (29), the difference between the mean (0.31) and the median is negligible. Still, Park was conscious of our warning regarding correlations and their non-computable nature. This is also true of Figure A5.6.

(i.e., alpha scores) for Perry's and Martin's tests are approximately the same, as are the distribution curves for these scores (i.e., monomodal and clustered in the center). Nevertheless, it is striking that the mean of Perry's distribution of interitem consistency scores is so much lower than that of Martin's alpha-if-item-deleted values. This is what we should expect, even if Perry's values were corrected upward to overcome their restriction due to rough grouping.

Which of these two measures should the researcher prefer? Probably the latter, especially at the beginning of the test construction process, when an instrument is still in its first draft and is raw and relatively untested. At that point, it is particularly important to see (as Perry's graph reveals) that certain items have a very meager average pull toward the instrument as a whole and are strong candidates for deletion, rewording, or other improvement.

What would we optimally hope for concerning the obtained distribution of interitem correlation? Probably a rather normal-shaped curve with a mean correlation (a corrected mean correlation, to be sure) of about 0.40 to 0.50. We would not want too many negative or extremely low mean interitem intercorrelation scores, because that would imply that such items tend to stand apart from the test as a whole. Perhaps these items pertain to dimensions that need to be measured separately, by instruments of their own. Perhaps they are items that are confusing to the subjects or that tend to be interpreted differently at different times or by different respondents. Conversely, we would also be wary of items that tended to intercorrelate extremely high (say 0.70 or over), on the average, with all other items. Such items should be examined for excessive redundancy. Given that we usually construct our instruments for research purposes in such a way that they will cover several different subcomponents that are nevertheless sufficiently interrelated to be clustered together, in additive fashion, we should aim for only a few average interitem correlation scores that are in the 0.70 range, with a mean that is not much above 0.50. (These recommended values are but rules of thumb we have learned through experience, not necessarily based on theoretical or scientific findings.)

So far we have looked at the distribution of mean difficulty scores and stressed the need for a balanced normal distribution of such scores for the entire test. We also considered ways to assess both the extent to which individual items contribute to the stability of the entire test and the extent to which each item correlates with the other items on the test. What we have left to do is to assess the internal validity of the instrument, before assessing its criterion validity. This we will do item by item.

Item Discriminability

Just as with item reliability, it pays for beginning researchers to familiarize themselves with the research literature in order to maximize the validity of each test item. An understanding of theories, models, and constructs as elements in the relationship between "the real thing" and the constructs represented in the test will enhance a researcher's ability to develop, choose, and refine the individual items that make up tests. The wording of each item ought to maximize the instrument's measuring power by minimizing ambiguity and complexity without giving away too much and eliciting "right" answers from subjects. Having said all this, whenever a more than adequate outside validity criterion or an independent approximation of the "real (overt or covert behavioral) thing" that we are trying to measure exists, it should not be too difficult to identify those items that correlate most substantially with it. For example, if we have independent mean ratings of subjects by specialists who are most familiar with the subjects, then each item's response can be correlated with the mean specialist rating for each subject on the overt or covert behavior. Unfortunately this situation is highly unlikely, particularly in the first draft stage of these developments—a reality that also contributes to the ultimate difficulties associated with satisfying criterion validity requirements in tests for research purposes. The difficulty involved in validating instruments as a whole also manifests itself while attempting to differentiate between the validity of individual items.

As if the foregoing problems were not enough, there is the additional problem that validity data for instruments is not usually gathered until the instruments are in their second or third versions. That only intensifies the issue of how to revise a test using data obtained pertaining to the item characteristics of the first version, including those characteristics that would maximize item validity. Obviously some compromise is needed that, if perhaps not entirely satisfactory to our most rigorous inclinations, does allow us to address essential validity concerns. Such a compromise ought to serve us throughout our item construction and item revision efforts, but especially during the early stages of our work.

The compromise that has been adopted in this area is based on an honest answer to the following question: "Supposing that the preliminary draft of our instrument were valid, what measure that derives from the test itself would be the best or fullest reflection of that validity?" Obviously, the answer is "The total score that our instrument yields." The total score, yielding much greater score variance than any of the items' scores, will hence yield the highest correlation with whatever our validity criterion might ultimately be.

If our test's total score is the most valid test-derived indicator that we have or can have before validation per se, then our initial expression of item validity can be the correlation of each item's responses with the total test score minus the score for the item in question. The validity of item 5, for example, can be expressed as the correlation between the answers to item 5, across all subjects, and the total scores obtained by these subjects minus their responses to item 5 (in order not to count item 5 twice, thereby spuriously elevating the correlation). This is exactly what is done in the item validity estimation procedure known as item discriminability. The statistic itself is provided directly in SPSS, where it is referred to as "corrected item total correlation." The "correlation" in this case is derived from the subtraction of the item response from the total score to which it has contributed.

As when calculating interitem consistency, the correlation involved is a straight Pearsonian r and therefore constitutes an underestimate of the true correlation. Again, rough grouping causes this underestimate. To overcome this underestimate, it would be necessary to utilize biserial (or point-biserial) correlations between replies to dichotomous items and total scores (minus those items), on the one hand, or "quadraserial" (or "quintiserial" or "sixtiserial") correlations between replies to four, five, or six option items and total scores (minus those items), on the other hand. Unfortunately, statistical packages do not commonly offer any of these correlations in their item statistic sections. Therefore, a corrected Pearsonian is all we can hope for concerning a corrected item total correlation.

What kind of distribution of item discriminabilities would we like to obtain, in the best of all possible worlds? A bell-shaped distribution with its mean as high as possible. We do not have to worry about the mean of the distribution of item discriminabilities being too high, because, as we have mentioned before, our recurring problem is that the validity scores we obtain are too low, instead of too high. Nevertheless, should we somehow obtain a negatively skewed curve with a mean in the nineties, we ought to be far from pleased. Such a result would indicate that our items and the total score were excessively redundant. In fact, instead of using the test as a whole, we could just as well use any one of the highly discriminating individual items and come to the same conclusions about our subjects as we would by using the entire test. Experience has demonstrated to us that a bell-shaped curve with its mean in the high 0.60s to low 0.80s is usually as good as it gets, and we should be happy, indeed, if that is what is obtained.

Let us look at two distributions of item discriminabilities that have been computed for items from the first version of tests developed by Martin and Perry. Figure A5.5, based on Martin's Medical Coping Instrument, shows quite a scatter of corrected item–total correlation scores, without any well-defined mode, and with individual items falling along a longish continuum from around –0.30 to around 0.70. The mean is 0.21, but given that the correlations are Pearsonian r's, the mean is really somewhat higher than that, perhaps approximately 0.33. (See note 3 for the correction factors corresponding to each number of item response categories.) Perry's item discriminability scores (figure A5.6), in developing her first version of the Fear of Cancer Self-Scrutiny test, also show quite a spread, approximately between 0.05 and 0.80. In this case, the median is at 0.55, and a clearer mode is in evidence, although the distribution as a whole is also far from normal.

Clearly, each investigator has discovered items that differ greatly in discriminability; therefore, each can decide to drop or revise or replace less well-designed items in the second version of the instruments that will be constructed. In deciding what to do with each item and before arriving at final decisions, one must take into consideration all three item analysis dimensions simultaneously (as will the subcomponential design of their respective instruments). Yet, item discriminability is the one dimension worthy of special consideration. We cannot stress enough the fact that instrument validity is the hardest asset to obtain or demonstrate. Its pursuit via item analysis is a major opportunity that must not be overlooked. We shall examine the specific issues and steps involved in first- and second-version decision making on these very three dimensions in chapters B4 and B5.

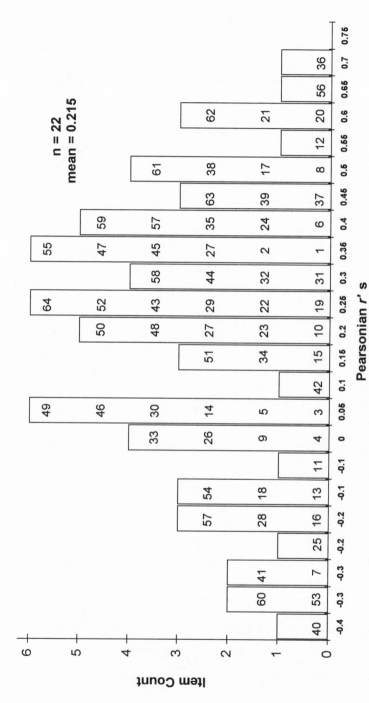

Figure A5.5. Martin's Item Discriminability Scores for the Medical Coping Instrument, Version 1 (MCI-1)

Note: Numbers in bars are item numbers.

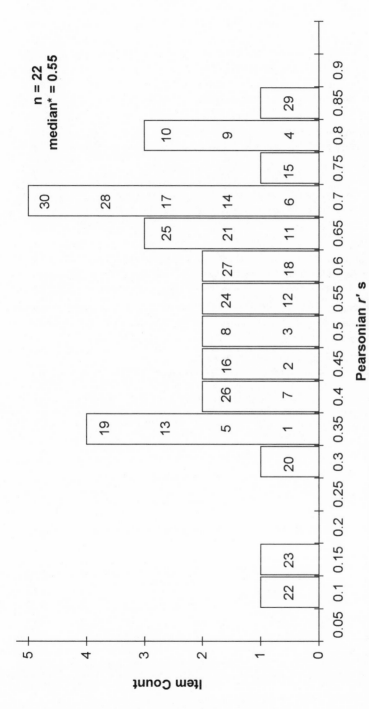

Figure A5.6. Perry's Item Discriminability Scores for the Fear of Cancer Self-Scrutiny Instrument, Version 1 (FCSSI-1)

Note: Numbers in bars are item numbers.

*Given the large number of items (30), the difference between the mean (0.52) and the median is negligible. Still, Park was conscious of our warning regarding correlations and their non-computable nature. This is also true of Figure A5.4.

Notes

1. Perry's items were counterbalanced for purposes of presentation to the subjects; that is, they were so formulated that for some items, the criterial direction was toward the left of the scale, and for other items, it was toward the right of the scale. However, for ease of scoring, some items were then "flipped" so that they could all be graphed in the same criterial direction. The same counterbalancing and "flipping" procedures were followed in connection with constructing, scoring, and graphing Martin's (and all other investigators') items. Counterbalancing is mentioned in chapter B2.

2. Strictly speaking, correlation coefficients are not numbers that can be averaged. Where the number of items is "small" (e.g., less than twenty), the appropriate statistic to use is the *median* interitem correlation. However, as the number of items increases, the difference between the mean and the median will decrease, so that with a large number of items the mean is more than adequate. Furthermore, it is usually far easier to obtain a mean than a median in most statistics programs.

3. See the discussion of "Correction in r for Errors of Grouping" Guilford (1956). For two, three, four, five, six, or seven categories (these being the usual number of categories that are employed in obtaining responses to items), the corrections are .30, .20, .11, .07, .05, and .04 respectively. Clearly, the greater the number of response categories, the less the grouping error that needs to be corrected for. Dichotomous items require the most substantial corrections, even when phi, biserial, or point-biserial correlations are calculated.

~

Sociopsychological Scales

Among the worrisome problems that plague the types of instruments we discuss in this book are the often low correlations between what respondents say in private (to their close friends and relatives) and what they say to outsiders (among them test constructors). Lower still are the correlations between what subjects say and what they do. Often these inconsistencies have been blamed on the lack of a real metric in Likert scales such as those we have focused on thus far. In other words, critics point to the arbitrariness of the words used to anchor the points in a scale as related to the attitude they attempt to measure.

This charge of a lack of metric is well founded, but whether this trait is responsible for the problems just indicated remains quite doubtful. Attitudes may be states rather than traits, and they may be constrained or governed by different situational circumstances in different contexts. Furthermore, attitudes are made up of systems of beliefs, emotions, and behaviors that are (1) changeable and not necessarily balanced and (2) mediated by the subject's intentions, which tend to depend for the most part on the particulars of the situation. (For a full discussion on ways to measure attitudes, see Henerson, Morris, and Fitz-Gibbon, 1987.) This makes the demonstration of their validity rather difficult. Nevertheless, the issue of a real metric deserves to be pondered in its own right.

Likert Scaling

Likert scales, named after Rensis Likert (1903–1981), share many fundamental characteristics with teacher-made spelling tests. Each word a student spells correctly typically earns the same number of points as does any other word on the test, regardless of its difficulty. Similarly, in Likert scales, every item has the same response options; therefore, a "fully agree" to one item earns the same number of credits as does a "fully agree" to any other item, regardless of interitem differences (i.e., degree of difficulty). As if that were not enough to cast aside all pretense as to a real metric, the lock-step weighting of the response options is also purely arbitrary. "Fully agree" differs from "agree more than disagree" by just as much as the latter does from "disagree more than agree" or than from any other option. These options may be along an ordinal scale, but they are typically treated as intervals or even ratios.

At best, the Likert scale is an intensity scale, with its total score being akin to the total score on a spelling test that measures overall goodness of spelling. Ten words correct is judged to be better than eight words correct; "fully agree" with eight items is judged to be worthy of a higher score than "agree more than disagree" with the same items. And just as the total spelling score does not tell us exactly which words the pupil spelled right and which ones he or she spelled wrong, so the total Likert-type score doesn't tell us with which items the subject "agreed fully," because intensity scores do not translate directly into substantive scores. A score of 75 on the spelling test still doesn't tell us whether *Mississippi* was spelled correctly, but it does imply a greater likelihood that it was spelled correctly by a student who received a score of 75 than is the case for a pupil who got a total score of 45. Picking items in accord with their discriminability indices has the same effect in Likert scale construction. Still, any given numerical score can be arrived at in a large number of different ways; therefore, no given score can really inform us of what exactly it is that subjects know or believe.

At this point, the reader may wonder why use Likert scales at all. Our answer is that the major argument on behalf of Likert scaling is not a metric argument at all, but a convenience argument. A large number of items can be rather easily written, tried out, revised, and tried out again, toward the goal of constructing scales of considerable reliability and, more often than not, substantial validity. In this sense, Likert scales resonate true to the spirit of mainstream American pragmatism: "If it works, it's good." But this view (one that is very facilitating, as far as most researchers are concerned) is not satisfying at all to those who are concerned about the fact that it provides neither a good metric for social research endeavors nor precise substantive indications to accompany the scores that it yields. Those who are of this persuasion, may turn either to Thurstone or to Guttman scaling for the construction of tests for research purposes. But, as is usual in life, one gains certain things and one loses certain things because of any choice that one makes. (The basic presentation of Likert's approach may be found in his 1932 monograph "A Technique for the Measurement of Attitudes," *Archives of Psychology, 140.*)

Thurstone Scaling

Louis Thurstone (1887–1955) provided an answer to the riddle that drove poor Gustave Fechner (1801–1887) mad. A rigorous physicist, psychologist, and philosopher, Fechner was convinced that psychology could never become a science in the "hard science" tradition so popular in Germany at the time, unless it solved the problem of devising true metrics for the behavioral phenomena that it studied. However, he was frustrated (and ultimately defeated) in his efforts by lack of appreciation for the concept of variance, a basic human sciences concept that is relatively absent in the physical sciences, which he used as a reference. In pursuit of the least noticeable difference as a unit of weight perception, Fechner was defeated by the fact that subjects did not agree not only with each other but not even with themselves on different occasions.

Half a century later, Thurstone was well aware of both variation between and within individuals, which is a basic tenet of the modern social and behavioral sciences. Thus, he was able to build upon this awareness in perfecting his ranking-linked method of equal appearing intervals. Thurstone scales are interval-level directional scales. A higher score indicates more of the phenomenon under study, and the units of "moreness" appear to be equal to judges who are like the subjects being studied. Both of these traits are clear improvements over the comparatively arbitrary nature of Likert scales. (For greater theoretical and procedural details, see Thurstone, 1929, or Thurstone & Chave, 1929.)

To construct a Thurstone scale, first one must generate a large number of items (approximately one hundred) to serve as indicators of a dimension of the variable or phenomenon in question. The underlying dimension may either go from a negative pole through neutrality to a positive pole, or deal entirely with positive items or entirely with negative items. Thus, Thurstone scales may be created to measure attitudes toward issues or topics that are either popular (e.g., children, sports, the environment) or unpopular (e.g., terrorism, sexual abuse, pollution). (For an example of a scale dealing entirely with negative items, see Fishman, 1955.) The wording of these items often covers the continuum of attitudes toward a particular referent (person, idea, issue, experience, or object). Examples of items drafted to capture the range of attitudes toward the Spanish language may include the following statements: "I like the sounds of words in Spanish," "I neither like nor dislike Spanish; it is just another language," and "Spanish is a dirty language."

The items are then sorted by ten to fifteen judges (or as many as possible) chosen from the same population for which the scale is intended. The judges work independently, assigning items into an odd number of categories (usually seven, nine, or eleven)[1] along an underlying scale of judged favorableness. Eventually, a set of chosen statements (i.e., items) will represent or express this scale. Judges may assign any number of statements to any particular category as long as they are of a roughly similar degree of favorableness and their decisions do not depend on other statements. Taking this approach avoids potential problems with items linked in such a way that their answer requires a previous item's answer (i.e., ipsativity). The mean for the judges' scale values for each item is computed, discarding items that elicit widely disparate ratings. Finally, two or three items are chosen for each category such that their mean scale values (1) fall within the category's interval and (2) have the smallest standard deviations. The items' scale value is the assigned interval's mean value, and their order on the scale is determined at random so as not to make obvious the dimension they represent.

The instructions for subjects completing the finished scale are to mark all the items that they agree with. Each subject's score is the mean weight of all the items that the subject agrees with. Since the interval assignments made by the initial scale-constructing judges determine the item weights, it is extremely important that these judges be drawn from the same population as the subjects to which the research results will be generalized. Judges have been found to display more within-group than between-group similarity in the item assignments that they make, with judges who are themselves characterized by extreme attitudes constantly skewing their item assignments much more than moderate judges do (Fishman and Lorge, 1954).

Though clearly more difficult to generate, Thurstone scales have advantages over Likert scales. Because every item carries its own weight, in accord with (1) the mean interval assignments and (2) the highest degree of consensus of the panel of judges, the mean weight of the items subscribed to by subjects have concrete meaning. Although the items are presented to subjects in random order, subjects actually tend to agree with items whose scale values are close together. For instance, when discussing a subject (or a group of subjects) with a mean score of 5.2, the researcher can then say that such a subject (or group) tends to agree with other scale items whose mean weight is around 5.2 and can mention the items that may be characterized accordingly. This is an improvement over two chief problems with Likert scores: all items are weighted equally, and the researcher cannot tell the subjects' responses to particular items from their total scores.

There are, however, serious problems with Thurstone scales. First, the statistics needed for item analyses and that we will describe in subsequent chapters can no longer be obtained. In Likert scaling, every subject responds to every item. In Thurstone scaling, subjects only indicate those items with which they agree. Such selective response patterns make it nearly impossible to compare items with each other precisely because they are not equally weighted. For this reason, it is quite difficult to determine the contribution to the instrument's reliability for each item, since the instrument lacks a total score from which to obtain a variance to be compared with that of the items. When it comes to assessing the reliability of an instrument in terms of interitem consistency, things become quite difficult. Respondents usually choose items with roughly equivalent weights. By definition, these items are likely to be inconsistent with other items, the more so the more distant the weights of the latter are from the weights of the items subscribed to.

Second, assessing the validity of a Thurstone scale with the method we describe in this book is even more problematic (or, frankly, impossible). Thurstone scales lack a total score with which item acceptances can be correlated. Both of the latter item statistics are essentially ruled out because responses to individual items are influenced by responses to other items, particularly between responses distant from those that respondents have already selected. Thus, subjects who are positive toward the referent of inquiry cannot accept the negative items on the scale due to the very fact that positiveness tends to rule out negativeness. Many researchers have concluded that the absence of meaningful item statistics is a high price to pay for the availability of a metric of equal appearing intervals. We tend to agree. Furthermore, constructing Thurstone scales demands considerable time and resources, a condition that goes counter to our aim of making test construction accessible to beginning researchers.

Guttman Scaling

Another method of providing a metric for items is the method perfected by Louis Guttman (1916–1987). Thurstone's metric derives from the category assignments of judges, whereas Guttman's metric derives from what the implications are for the subjects' responses. Guttman scales have the advantage that a single score allows researchers to predict patterns of response for all the items on the scale. Moreover, when the Guttman scale represents a single dimension, scores can be thought of as moving from general to specific. Though the items on the scale may or may not appear in order, a positive response (i.e., acceptance, agreement) toward a specific item presupposes acceptance of more general items.

Guttman scales are characterized by the "implicational" or "scalable" nature of their items. Correspondingly, tasks that can be successfully completed only when their component subtasks or preconditions are completed in a given order are said to be "implicational" or "scalable" in nature. If one is informed that the student reached step 6, one can be sure that he or she had reached steps 5, 4, 3, 2, and 1 as well. Some fields of knowledge are implicational (e.g., calculus assumes trigonometry, which assumes algebra, which assumes arithmetic). The beauty of Guttman scaling is that its final scores are equivalent to the highest (i.e., most extreme, most advanced) item that subjects have agreed with or answered correctly, and from that score we immediately know all the other items that the subject has agreed with or answered correctly. That score itself implies or presupposes all the others. When this condition exists, the scale is said to be perfectly or fully scalable or implicational.

In the attitudinal domain, some attitudes are scalable as well. In table A6.1, items 2 through 6 scale perfectly, but item 7 is only 83 percent scalable, since from the responses to it one can predict the responses to only five of the six other items. In other words, not everyone who answered

Table A6.1. Perfect and Less Than Perfect Item Scalability

Items Answered	Items Implied							% Implicational
	1	2	3	4	5	6	7	
1	—							100
2	*	—						100
3	*	*	—					100
4	*	*	*	—				100
5	*	*	*	*	—			100
6	*	*	*	*	*	—		100
7	*	*	*	—	*	*	—	83

item 7 "right" also answered the other items "right." Therefore, the scale is not perfectly implicational.

Guttman set very high standards in this connection and would have rejected a scale such as the one represented in table A6.1. It is quite difficult to assemble Guttman scales that are perfectly scalable and with more than a few items in length. Out of a total initial item pool of dozens of items, only a subset of a half dozen or so will be perfectly scalable. This may be a problem since that subscale may not be a full or representative sample of the total universe of knowledge, attitude, or behavior being studied (see Guttman, 1950).

To construct a Guttman scale, one begins with between twenty and thirty statements that apply to the research topic and a large sample (fifty to one hundred) of respondents from the target population. From here on, the scale is constructed through a process of elimination. First, one eliminates statements that elicit 80 percent or more of acceptance or rejections from the respondents. Next, after rank-ordering respondents from high to low acceptance rates, one eliminates statements that fail to discriminate between contrasting (high/low) respondents. From here on, the question of whether the items are scalable or whether the scale as a whole is implicational becomes an empirical one. The goal is to obtain reproducibility scores (obtained by dividing number of consensual agreements over total number of items) of 0.85 or higher.

As was true for Thurstone scales, where items are selected for inclusion by criteria that pertain only to such scales and to no others, Guttman scale items cannot be selected by the item analyses criteria related to Likert-type items, which we have described in detail in previous chapters. Considerations of item difficulty, interitem consistency, and item discriminability simple do not apply to Guttman scale items, where items are accepted to maximize scalability and for no other property. The pursuit of their particular metrics, intellectually gratifying though such a pursuit may be, exacts another price as well. Furthermore, regardless of how high a reproducibility score one manages to obtain for any given scale, this alone does not guarantee that the scale actually measures the variable of interest. Let us not forget that validity, together with reliability, should figure prominently in the minds of test constructors.

Thurstone scales may or may not be more difficult to construct than Likert scales. In contrast, Guttman scales are definitely more difficult to construct than either of the others, but both Thurstone and Guttman scales clearly tend to be somewhat less reliable and somewhat less valid than Likert scales. This is a direct consequence of their greater brevity, particularly in the case of the Guttman scales. As a result, most investigators prefer to construct Likert scales, and if the pursuit of a metric is of great importance to them, they convert their Likert scores to standard scores (i.e., to simple z or deviation scores).

Perhaps the lesson to be learned from all of this is that it is not the elegance of the metric that counts in social and psychological research; rather, it is the degree to which criteria of significance can be accounted for. As long as that remains the criterion of a successful measure—and so it should remain even for attitude research—then there would seem to be little to be gained from elegant metrics of any kind.

We close this chapter by warning the reader that our discussion of attitude measurement is intended *only for initial orientational and contrastive purposes* (vis-à-vis Likert scaling). It is not by itself adequate preparation for the construction of either Thurstone or Guttman scales. If interested in developing such scales, the reader is well advised to read more extensive treatments, such as those we list among the recommended readings in appendix A.

Note

1. Notice that this recommendation is different from the one we offer regarding Likert scale items in chapter B1. With Likert scales, we recommend using an even number of response choices to reduce the tendency among responders to choose the seemingly neutral middle option. However, for Thurstone scales, it is desirable for judges to have an odd number of categories available. This allows them to be as accurate as possible in rating individual items, including those items deemed to be in the middle of the range.

~

EMPIRICAL TOPICS

In this section, we focus on the procedural and practical aspects of test construction for research purposes. We begin by addressing concerns related to the selection of the items that make up the test. We stress the importance of building construct validity into our instruments by ensuring that the items we choose represent all the relevant components of the behavior we intend to study. As part of this process, we point to the need to develop items that not only reduce the possibility of experimental error and test bias but also avoid common structural problems related to ipsativity, or the dependence of some items' scores on previous items' scores. We also discuss measures that maximize the potential of either individual items or measures or both to capture nonspurious variance.

The next step in the process consists of assembling what will be the first version of the test, which includes, among other things, the formatting of items and of the instrument as a whole. Once the first version of the test is ready, we recommend pilot-testing it before proceeding to a formal evaluation of all items. In pilot-testing the instrument, the aim is to identify potentially troublesome items or procedural issues before investing much time and effort during the formal evaluation phase and, obviously, before collecting data. The formal evaluation, in turn, includes evaluating both individually and together each item's difficulty, consistency, and discriminability scores, as well as the instrument's overall reliability. Depending on the decision reached after examining their difficulty, consistency, and discriminability scores, each item is deleted, replaced, modified, or kept unchanged. The goal of this evaluation is the development of a second version of the test from the original version. This cycle (evaluation, revision, and reevaluation) may be repeated as many times as necessary and possible. However, unless their resources are vast, we expect that most researchers will only be able to put their instruments through two cycles.

It is worth repeating that, regardless of how many times the instrument is refined, its ultimate evaluation will depend on the extent to which the test's total score contributes to explain the variance of an external criterion. Figure Part B.1 depicts an outline of the steps involved in designing and developing at least a test's first and second version, as well as testing its external validity.

The practical and accessible nature of this book exemplifies our belief in the power of authentic experiences in learning. To that end, we encourage the reader to develop his or her own test and evaluate it using the approach we describe. We also realize that, for various circumstances, it may not be feasible to do just that. For this reason, we have included in appendix C an example of a set of items and item scores; we want to provide the reader with an opportunity to practice the procedures we describe.

After describing in detail the steps involved in evaluating and refining a test for research purposes, we conclude part B by exploring other varieties of semiformal measurement that depend, for the most part, on one form or another of content analysis. We follow this with a discussion of the potential benefits (and downfalls) of preparing a third version of the test and of further quantitative analyses that are possible.

Important principles, ideas, and concepts inform the approach to test construction for research purposes that we advocate. Yes, this book is practical, but to paraphrase Kurt Lewin's timeless admonition, there is nothing more practical than a good theory. It is with this in mind and to enhance the usefulness of our text when used to teach a course that we provide a summary of pertinent theory at the beginning of each chapter in this section. We encourage the reader to keep these in mind while performing the required analyses and revisions of the instrument. We have found that it is necessary to approach test construction with a clear understanding of validity, reliability, and related notions to be able to solve unexpected problems and complications that arise in the test construction process. Conversely, one's understanding of the theory of test construction benefits greatly from the practice of test construction in real and meaningful contexts.

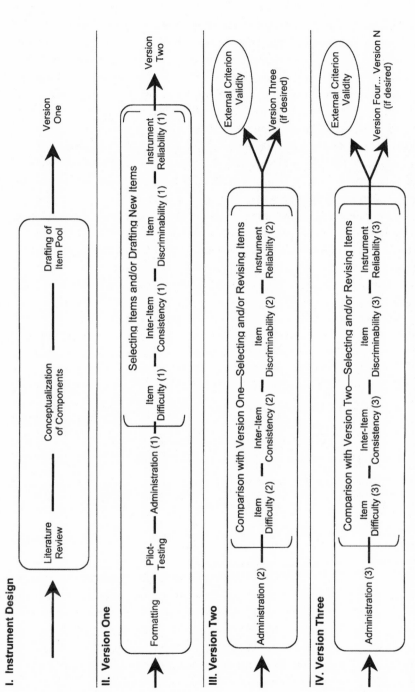

Figure B.1. Item and Instrument Development, Analyses, and Refinement, Including Criterion Validity Assessment

Finally, this is perhaps the most appropriate point in this guide for a simple yet valuable piece of advice that may seem obvious but is still worth mentioning: Test constructors and researchers in general ought to develop the habit of keeping a researcher's log with meticulous records about all aspects of the project. Such records may range from ideas about possible subcomponents of the phenomenon arising from observations or readings, to reactions and comments from informants to specific items, to decision rules regarding the labeling and coding of item scores onto a spreadsheet. All this information is too important to trust to memory, and keeping a researcher's log is a good habit for beginning researchers to develop even when dealing with small-scale field research projects. (For additional insights and considerations on data collection and management, especially of large-scale research projects, we refer the reader to Stouthammer-Loeber and van Kammen's [1995] *Data Collection and Management*.)

~

Designing Your Instrument: Componentiality and Item Type

As we have emphasized already, validity is the ultimate goal of test construction for research purposes. We also need to remind the reader of the various forms that validity takes in the context of test construction for research purposes. The design of a valid test depends, especially at first, on a clear understanding of relevant research literature. The researcher interested in developing a test for research purposes must be fully aware of the phenomenon, at least as described in the research literature. Thus, it pays to develop an instrument with both internal and external validity that are built incrementally with each subsequent version. It is also important to consider at these early stages any demographics that may shed light into the investigation, particularly since these variables must be included in the instrument from its earliest stages.

An early consideration in the process of test construction for research purposes—and, by implication, in undertaking a research project—is to determine whether the particular research question is about something that exists in nature, the "real thing," so to speak. Furthermore, even if such "real thing" exists, is it possible to measure its existence? We recognize that there are nonquantifiable "real things" worth investigating, but at least for the approach to research we embrace in this book, a test's external validity can only be determined if it is measured. Especially for beginning researchers using tests for research purposes, the external validity of the instruments used is key in ensuring that the data they will eventually collect with their instruments originates in a real world phenomenon rather than in their enthusiastic thinking about the research problem.

One question ought to be present in the mind of test constructors especially at the onset of the test construction process: "How will I demonstrate the external validity of my instrument?" In addition to a measurable external criterion, experts' consensus, previously validated tests, and consensually contrasted groups, or a combination of these and demographic variables are ways to build a test's incremental validity.

Regarding the nature of the scales used in formal measurement, one of the markers of a successful researcher is a healthy dose of pragmatism. As such, Likert scales, though not truly scales in the strictest sense of the word, offer the best option for beginning researchers.

Finally, we must say a word about formal measurement and quantitative analyses: We expect the reader to have at least a basic understanding of correlation and its close cousin, regression, as ways of expressing a linear relation between two variables. For it is in being able to quantify a linear relationship between two variables that a test constructor can estimate a test's external validity. If any of the points mentioned in this brief summary are not clear, we suggest that the reader refer to chapters A2 and A4 for a review of the theory behind the procedures described in this chapter. In addition, we suggest that the reader review the discussion about sociopsychological scales in chapter A6.

Componentiality

No instrument to be used for research purposes should be constructed without a thorough familiarity with the research literature on the substantive field with which the research deals. This admonition may sound so trite as not to deserve repeating, but it is repeated here only because of the deleterious measurement consequences of lack of such familiarity. Our research should seek to stand on the shoulders of earlier researchers, be they giants or not. Research, as any form of inquiry, ought to be a cumulative enterprise in which past findings suggest future areas of research by bringing to the surface lacunae in our understanding of the phenomena in question. This is often true even of research that either did not prove a hypothesis or did not ask exactly the same substantive question.

Another reason to base our research on past research is also quite practical: Past research inevitably suggests the probable componentiality of any instrument we may wish to construct. No one today would undertake to measure intelligence without taking into account the several different kinds or components of intelligence that previous research has demonstrated and documented. Similarly, even when conducting research in far less explored fields than intelligence, researchers need to conceptualize the components of the phenomenon under study before engaging in the development of a test to research the phenomenon. Especially in these days of readily accessible information and exploding research in all fields, rarely does the conceptualization of the components that make up a particular focus of study need to be de novo.

No matter how novel a research field or topic may be, it is still necessary for a researcher to wonder, "Who, before me, found or suggested substantive subcomponents of the phenomenon that I wish to measure and that I should be sure to try to build into my own measure?" Even if the researcher's conceptualization of the phenomenon is so novel that no previous research is directly linked to this new approach, researchers often are still able to obtain substantive subcomponents from research on similar phenomena or phenomena that may influence the one in question. Giving sufficient thought to matters such as these, and doing so the earliest along in the process of instrument construction, will help obviate that sinking feeling in one's stomach that comes when someone listening to your results says, "But you forgot to build such-and-such component into your measure. And so-and-so's research has already indicated that one shouldn't really overlook *that* when trying to measure the very behavioral or attitudinal construct that you are trying to measure, because including it is much more productive in trying to account for the criterion of such-and-such than ignoring it."

Let us once more use our former students' work to illustrate componentiality in test construction. When Glazer started to construct an instrument to measure how people cope with medical problems, her review of other literature on coping with stresses suggested four possible components that should be provided for: (1) proactive behavioral, (2) proactive cognitive, (3) reactive behavioral, and (4) reactive cognitive. Similarly, in the winter of 1996, Metcalf undertook to construct an instrument for measuring the degree of acceptance among voters toward legislation being considered by the U.S. Congress that would require the use only of English in any communication from or to the federal government. Metcalf's review of the literature suggested that he should build into his measure components dealing with (1) extent of respondent information about the English-only issue, (2) liberal versus conservative social and political attitudes more generally, and (3) demographic features that might presuppose respondents to take either side of this issue (ethnicity, political party preference, and age among others). However, both Glazer and Metcalf also wanted to derive a single total score from their instrument, rather than three or four subscores to be used as separate predictors of some criterion of coping or of favoring an English-only position. Thus, their underlying assumption was really that their components all correlated positively with each other and did so to such a degree that they could safely yield a single total score, rather than three or four necessarily separate scores. In other words, the components were assumed to be identifiably *separate parts of a basically unitary underlying phenomenon*, coping with stress, on the one hand, and favoring an English-only position, on the other.

How can components be both separate enough to have to be provided for adequately when designing the instrument yet related enough to each other to be added together into one total score? The answer is that they have to be more related than separate *concerning the criterion that we are trying to predict or explain*. Height and weight are both important considerations in normal human development *and* have a positive relationship one to the other. Nevertheless, it is almost unheard of to have a total height-plus-weight score. We all know enough short and heavy people and tall and lean people to render such a total score less meaningful or useful than either separate scores or conjoint scores (weight at a given height). On the other hand, Scholastic Aptitude Test (SAT) scores are often totaled, even though separate Verbal (SAT-V) and Mathematical (SAT-M) sections exist, to yield a total Verbal + Mathematical score. Some people may have a strong verbal aptitude and a weak mathematical aptitude (or vice versa). Yet, both aptitudes commonly go together and, consequently, correlate substantially with each other, so that adding the two scores together is a very useful thing to do *in predicting the criterion that most selective colleges have in mind* (grade point average at the end of the freshman year in college) when they are trying to decide which candidates to admit. Apparently, academic aptitude in the freshman year in many American colleges is a more unitary trait than is human development, and, accordingly, it can be better predicted by a unitary test score totaled across two of its components (Verbal + Mathematical scores) than can human development vis-à-vis two of its components (height + weight).

So, how did Glazer and Metcalf know whether the components that they were building into their instruments where like height and weight or whether they were like SAT-V and SAT-M? Well, they did not know for sure, at the outset. Their reading of the relevant literatures led them to make a bet that they were dealing with separate components that were, nevertheless, basically more like SAT-V and SAT-M than like height and weight and, therefore, that these components could be given separate attention while constructing their instruments and yet be subsequently totaled together into a single overall total score.

Obviously, constructing tests for research purposes involves more than placing bets. Specifically, both Glazer and Metcalf were able to assess the soundness of their decisions using data. If their choice of components was erroneous, then these subsequent results would clearly indicate that. At that point, the decision must be made of whether to build one instrument alone or more than one, each based on the separate components identified and each yielding a separate score of its own. If the latter approach were to be followed, it might eventually lead to using a battery of tests to predict a single criterion. In that case, the tests would still have to be constructed one at a time, and each of them would still be developed in accord with the principles and procedures described in this book.

Finally, along with the single-total score approach or the battery or multiple-test approach to constructing tests for research purposes, there is also the even more highly multifaceted questionnaire approach. We only mention questionnaires from time to time, since a full appreciation of such an approach requires detailed treatment in its own right. In brief, when using a questionnaire for research, *each question may be viewed as tapping a completely separate dimension in the prediction of responses to a given criterion, and no total score is utilized or obtained across all of these dimensions.* (For those interested in a full discussion of the theoretical and technical aspects involved in using questionnaires for research, we recommend Robert Peterson's [1999] *Constructing Effective Questionnaires.*)

A discussion of componentiality in test construction would not be complete without mention of factor analysis involving individual item or scales scores. In chapter B2, we describe the types of item analyses that we believe are necessary to develop a test for research purposes. Yet, the reader will notice that we make no mention of factor analysis.[1] Our position regarding the use of factor analysis in relation to componentiality in tests is that they serve primarily a confirmatory purpose. Only after careful consideration of an instrument's various forms of internal validity and systematic refinement of individual items can a factor analysis help us either confirm or question our theoretical understanding of the phenomenon in question. We favor approaching a research question with a carefully articulated conceptual framework that informs the entire process of developing, evaluating, and refining test items and scales that correspond to the components included in the phenomenon of interest. Instead, all too often we have seen factor analysis used in "fishing expeditions" intended to flesh out partially developed conceptual frameworks or models. The risks implicit in such practices, particularly with large population samples, should become obvious when one remembers that factor analysis is, at its core, correlational in nature. Conversely, there are limits to the usefulness of factor analysis in small samples such as those most likely to be used by readers of this guide.

Item Characteristics

One must never forget that in the one-total-score approach to constructing tests for research purposes, instruments and their total scores are derived from items. Constructing an instrument for research purposes entails constructing, evaluating, and revising it on an item-by-item basis. Part B focuses on this very process. Of course, we will ultimately be concerned with certain crucial indicators of our instrument as a whole (primarily reliability and validity), but these indicators, too, are the by-products of our item-by-item success or failure during instrument construction.

So, what kinds of items do we want? Obviously our items should be well written so that they are easily understood. In other words, our instruments should not be reading tests; quite the contrary, we want to be sure that readability is *not* a major determinant of total score. Our test items should also be unambiguous, inoffensive, and not conducive to answering behaviors that are more related to total score than they are to the *ultimate criteria* that we are trying to predict. A common group of answering behaviors of the latter kind includes those that originate in the subjects' concern for giving an appearance that is favorable to their own self concept. "Fake-good" and social desirability responses fall under this group of answering behaviors, and test constructors must take pains not to elicit them.

Another category of answering behaviors that present problems for test building concerns item bias. Such bias, be it of gender, socioeconomic status, ethnic, or racial origin, usually produces opposite results: biased items artificially lower or inflate test performance in comparison to criterion performance. It, too, must be guarded against in tests for research purposes. The stakes for answering behavior resulting from social desirability or item bias pressures increase greatly when dealing with operational tests.

It bears repeating that, whenever test scores are used to significantly impact individuals' lives, test constructors and users must be especially vigilant for any indications of test bias of any sort.

In addition to these content characteristics of items, there are also certain structural characteristics of items that we should try to either avoid or foster. Among the structural characteristics to avoid are (1) ipsativity and (2) loss of variance in elicited item response through inappropriate grouping of responses. Ipsativity occurs when and to the degree that later item responses are constrained by earlier item responses. While it may be possible to accommodate a small number of funneling items (e.g., "If you have answered yes to item 15, go on to item 16, but if you have answered no, go on to item 17"), a large number of such items will seriously limit the instrument. This is because one of the basic assumptions in tests (at least in tests for research purposes such as we have discussed so far) is that each item has been answered substantially independently of all other items and their answers. Also, ipsative are items that provide several options but ask respondents to number these options according to preference. An example of such an item may be one that asks students to rank school subjects by assigning them a number (e.g., 1 = lowest, 10 = highest). Finally, items that require subjects to assign a certain number of responses of a given type to a prespecified number of items should also be avoided. For instance, asking hospital patients to match items from two columns, one that focuses on physician's behaviors and the other on patients' feelings, would present problems as far as being able to apply the methods we propose for item analyses.

All the item types mentioned share a common characteristic: responses to some items are more constrained than are the responses to other items, or, to put it another way, the responses to items are neither maximally nor equally independent of each other. In item construction, mutual independence of items should be our constant goal. Indeed, if it were possible for us to do so, we would really like to present all items in a different random order to each respondent in order to counteract the constant conditioning of subsequent items by previous items. Usually, paper-and-pencil measures for research purposes cannot really attain the goal of generating a different randomized presentation of items to every subject, though with recent increases in the use of computerized tests, this may become the norm soon. The one definite precaution that can be observed, however, is that ipsative items per se not be built into our instruments.

Ipsativity exists in such well-known instruments as the Allport-Vernon (1970) Scale of Values, Q-sort instruments,[2] and various occupational preference instruments. Although many of these instruments are theoretically intriguing, strictly speaking, the complete ipsativity of their items renders them noncomparable to other instruments in terms of all the item and instrument statistics that are usually utilized for purposes of measurement construction, selection, or revision.

The other item characteristic that we should avoid is that which forces respondents to provide either excessively gross or excessively refined response choices. Excessively gross item responses, such as asking respondents to make fewer distinctions between response options than they would or could readily make, will reduce item response variance. Items that yield responses with negligible variance provide us with limited information to decide their fate, regardless of the centrality of the component tapped by these items. Variance is, indeed, one of our prime concerns, whether it be about item responses, total score distributions, or criterion prediction. In each case, we are trying to account for or explain variance in human behavior, and, to be able to do so, we must have variance to work with in the first place.

To be able to determine the extent to which variance on one item or variable is related to variance on others, we must be able to measure variance and to predict it. Not letting the variance that is present in human behavior come to the fore would be like trying to account for the variance in basketball success without allowing the variance in height or in speed to be expressed or captured by our performance data. If every player is six feet tall (or even ten feet tall), height will not come through as a factor related to basketball success. The same will be true for an item or for an instrument that does not allow the real underlying variance in human responses to come through.

While one must allow for all the relevant variance in our subjects to come through in the tests we design, we must also avoid building spurious variance into our instruments at all costs. Asking subjects to select among ten response options to all items is probably requesting them to make more distinctions than they either are able or care to make. A truer appreciation of the importance of height in basketball success is not gained by measuring player height in millimeters rather than in inches. Thus, it is *true variance* (rather than error variance) that we are trying to tap, and neither too gross nor too refined measures will contribute to that much desired goal.

How does one know initially how refined to make one's items? Well, initially one does not know, really. We normally give our respondents no more than four or six response options per item[3] (but sometimes as few as two) and then scrutinize our item statistics (see chapter B4) to determine whether too little or too much response variance seems to be in evidence. Since many of the initial items we design may suffer in one way or another, it is good to start out with a much larger item pool than is ultimately required. In this way, the attrition that the pool will experience will not destroy the subcomponential structure of the final instrument that we are aiming at. Throughout the investigation, but particularly during the initial item construction phase of the process, it is particularly helpful to collaborate with fellow researchers interested in similar research topics. An even better alternative is to embark in collaborative research, for it is in brainstorming sessions with colleagues who share a general understanding of the components that make up the research phenomenon that the potential exists for generating extensive pools of initial items.

As implied earlier, we will be concerned with two item response types: (1) dichotomous and (2) more than dichotomous or continuous. *Dichotomous* items are of the yes/no, true/false, sometimes/never, or agree/disagree variety. Response options such as these provide only for a single, simple, all-or-none distinction. However, if it is possible for subjects to make finer between several degrees of intensity, frequency, agreement, or other response continuum, then it is to our advantage to enable them to do so. This will enable us to better recognize valid distinctions that exist between individuals, which might not be recognizable, or as recognizable, from dichotomous items alone. Whenever we measure real variance (i.e., real differences between individuals on the dimension being measured), our instruments are stronger and tend to perform better. This is particularly so when respondents use all of the response options provided, rather than just a few. Any clustering of responses to a particular item will reduce variance on that item, which might lead us to conclude that it is not functioning well and should be deleted or redesigned. Thus, we must constantly *try both to maximize whatever response variance really exists, as well as not to introduce spurious or random variance that is unrelated to criterion variance*.

Obviously, there is a fine balance between providing for sufficient variance and safeguarding against spurious excessive variance. Therefore, every instrument has to go through several versions to successfully attain this delicate balance. Instrument construction is not an easy or rapid-fire undertaking. It takes time, patience, experience, luck, and skill. At the applied level, the journey begins with deciding about subcomponents and item types. The initial decisions in these connections may be either wrong or somewhat wrong and somewhat right. They will never be entirely right. The test construction process is essentially a procedure for focusing on demonstrably better definitions of both subcomponentiality and items.

Notes

1. Factor analysis is a way to find out, from the available set of item scores, which items and/or scales go together and the extent to which they do so. For readers interested in learning more about factor analysis, we refer them to the very readable and enjoyable essay by Connie Stapleton we list in appendix A.

2. Q-sorts are the central element in a research methodology invented by the British physicist and psychologist William Stephenson (1902–1989). In general, Q methodology offers a way to systematically study subjectivity by having subjects assign a set of opinion statements into a fixed number of spaces along a fixed number of categories. This arrangement forces a normal distribution in the categorization of statements (usually ranging from "agree" to "disagree"). Since the placement of any one statement depends on the placement of other statements, Q-sorts present test constructors with ipsativity problems.

3. It is preferable to use an even number of options to minimize any tendency among informants to hide in the safe, neutral middle option. Such hiding tends to constrain response variance, which is something that test makers ought to avoid at all costs. Regardless of how many response options are chosen, our advice is to keep these the same for all Likert scale items. Having equivalent response scores greatly simplifies the item analyses process.

~

Preparation and Preliminary
Testing of the First Version

No matter how experienced the researcher, no one can rush directly into the final form of an instrument to be used for research purposes. Every research project explores *terra incognita* and therefore requires questions that have not been asked before (at least not in the same way or of the same subjects as those that a new research project addresses). In this chapter, we begin by considering what we believe are important factors influencing the content of the preliminary items and the format of the test. We then recommend that, prior to its first administration, a preliminary version of the test be put through a dry run using a representative sample of the population for which it is ultimately intended. Besides noticing potential problems, the goal of this dry run should be to uncover undesirable *and* desirable circumstances or outcomes not apparent up to this point in the process.

In embarking in the preliminary testing of the test's first version, and as we stated at the beginning of the previous chapter, we encourage the reader to think about validity as the driving concern in test construction. Being able to distinguish between internal (i.e., construct validity and content validity) and external (i.e., criterion validity) sources of validity will enhance the overall validity of the instrument. Similarly, in the decision-making process leading up to the dry run of their instruments, researchers must be cognizant of their understanding of the research phenomenon and possible, verifiable ways of measuring it. In selecting the dry run sample, and to the extent that these variables may contribute to the test's incremental validity, consideration should be given to the demographic composition of the sample. However, since reliability will define the uppermost limit of a test's validity, we encourage the reader to keep it in mind throughout the test construction process, but especially during the preliminary testing phase.

By now we hope that the reader has an appreciation for and an understanding of reliability as the capacity of an instrument to resist error variance, or the typical "wobbling" of scores across applications.

It is worth remembering that a test's validity can be no higher than its reliability. Thus, we discuss in chapter B3 three possible ways by which to measure a test's reliability. First, it is possible to measure differences in the scores of a test administered twice to the same sample. Second, it is also possible to administer two different but equivalent versions of a test. Finally, it is possible to compare the scores from two different halves of the test. Rather than the particulars of each one of these approaches, we hope that the reader understands the basic assumptions behind reliability and its evaluation.

We also want the reader to remember that there are a number of contributing factors to the "wobbling" of test scores between subsequent applications or even within a single application. These include extraneous variables, such as fatigue, stress, and distracters, and it is the responsibility of test constructors to consider these as they develop tests for research purposes. Reliability concerns are especially relevant in the development of operational tests that have high stakes for test takers.

Finally, if the reader has not yet thought about the use of scales in his or her test, this is as good a time as ever to do so. At the same time, we need to voice the need to be practical rather than dogmatic throughout the entire process. The final test ought to represent a balanced compromise of principles and important concerns with real-world applicability. An expanded discussion of the issues in this brief summary can be found in chapter A3 (reliability), chapter A4 (validity), and chapter A6 (scales).

We also want to reiterate the need to document observations and decisions related to test development in a researcher's log. Especially at this early point in the process, we encourage the reader to make habitual and detailed observation entries. Although observing the reactions of subjects to test items is far from being a systematic and objective assessment of the instrument's format, reliability, or validity, these observations will be useful in deciding the ultimate fate of individual items later on.

Preliminary Item Pool and Instrument Format

Despite the unique nature of every research project, there is some generalizable carryover from the previous instrument construction experiences that prior researchers have had. Among the lessons one learns from earlier instrument construction efforts is that it pays to begin with a large item pool. Indeed, it is advisable to begin with many more items than the number one would ultimately expect to use. Throughout the analysis, selection, and refinement of items (See chapters A5, B3, B4, and B6) leading up to the final version of the test, we will discard a large proportion of items that do not meet particular criteria. To ensure that the componentiality of the test is preserved, we recommend beginning with at least fifteen items for every component of the test. Similarly, since one would not want this attrition to completely decimate one subdimension or another, it is best to build in quite a bit of slack into every subdimension so that each of them will still have a good chance of weathering the inevitable attrition among the initially formulated items. Having spare items will enable us to close our item analyses with a better chance of having enough items for a revised draft or second version stage, and to make sure that the initially conceptualized componential structure has a fair chance to emerge reasonably intact.

But before one builds a large item pool, one must be able to formulate them such that they are not only appropriately worded but also balanced in their potential for both maximum desirable real variance and minimum undesirable spurious variance (discussed in the previous chapter). We offer the following twelve questions that every prospective instrument constructor should review concerning every item being written:[1]

Questions to Ask Yourself about Every Item You Write for an Instrument

1. *Why do I want to know this?* Do not include items that do not serve a specific research purpose, do not contribute to one or another of your componential subdimensions, or appeal to you for vague reasons, such as "Just because I thought that it might prove interesting."

2. *Does the question contain more than one idea?* Two-pronged questions are likely to be confusing to your respondents; they may elicit two responses that may leave respondents in a quandary and lead to item analysis results that prompt dropping such items.

3. *Does the question use abbreviations or words that may be unfamiliar to respondents?* Our research may be derived from a literature with a specialized terminology that is mostly unknown to the full variety of respondents we intend to study. Insofar as possible, all questions should be stated in language that is easily accessible to all potential respondents. Our instruments should not be reading tests, intelligence tests, or guessing games, particularly when neither reading skills, nor intelligence, nor guessing skills are the objects of our research.

4. *Is the question clear and unambiguous? Do any words have a double meaning?* Sometimes, words have one meaning to the lay public and another meaning to researchers or specialists. If samples from both populations are to be studied, the questions must be equally clear and unambiguous to both groups.

5. *Does the respondent have the knowledge and information to answer the question?* Questions that elicit a large proportion of "don't know" responses will later self-destruct during item analysis. All questions need to elicit answers rather than nonanswers, or they will fall by the wayside during the item analyses stage.

6. *Does the wording imply either an answer that the researcher favors or an answer that prompts a socially desirable response?* Researchers always have a particular hypothesis that they are testing. The questions you ask should neither favor nor penalize that hypothesis, nor should they enable respondents to "fake-good" by picking responses that erroneously enhance their own self-image.

7. *Will the question, as worded, embarrass or anger the respondent?* Questions that respondents would rather not answer truthfully prompt avoidance responses or either "don't know" or "no response" answers. All such responses and answers undercut the validity of these items and, predictably, lead to their elimination at the item analysis stage.

8. *Is the item redundant?* A few redundant items are sometimes unavoidable and may actually help build instrument reliability (see chapter A3). Too many such items are annoying to the respondents and suggest that the researcher has not taken the time to edit the scale before foisting it on the public.

9. *Is the item too long?* Long items pose problems insofar as readability and understandability are concerned. They often need to be read more than once by innocent respondents who are busy and want to get on with whatever other business they were engaged in before we asked for their assistance. Moreover, even after reading long items twice, many respondents are often not sure what is being asked of them by such items, a condition that undermines the instrument's validity—remember, our tests cannot be tests of reading skills.

10. *Are the response options mutually exclusive and adequate to cover every conceivable response?* When we finally locate cooperative respondents—which is not usually the simplest thing to do, anyway—it is a pity to waste their goodwill on either questions that do not permit them to tell us what they really have on their minds or response options that force them to choose a less than adequate answer.

11. *Are the response options counterbalanced and equally balanced between positive and negative options?* Subjects can often figure out which end is up or which response options contribute most to what they see as the "right answer" for the test. For this reason, it is a good idea to state about a quarter of the questions in such a way that the responses most agreeing with the particular external criterion are at the other end of the scale than is usually the case. This will require that the respondents read all questions more carefully. Additionally, the researcher should take care not to use items in such a way that positiveness and negativeness toward the referent of our research cannot be indicated equally readily by our respondents.

12. *Are the response options clear and unambiguous?* All other things being equal, try to give your respondents more rather than fewer response options, thereby increasing score variance, but do not give them so many options, or so finely differentiated options, that they cannot clearly and *reliably* distinguish between them.

Even after examining every potential item in accord with these twelve criteria, it is still impossible to avoid including at least some items that function poorly and that ultimately need to be dropped or rewritten, at least insofar as our particular subjects are concerned. That is why it is so advisable to start out with a substantial item pool, one that will enable you to simply drop poorly functioning items as well as preserving the conceptual integrity of your research.

Now, we come to a brief consideration of the issues of item and instrument format. First, much of what we recommend here is greatly dependent on context. Asking a person in the street to answer "a few questions" differs greatly from handing out a self-administered instrument to a classroom full of high school students (with the approval of their teacher or principal, of course). Obviously, the person in the street may not even care to acknowledge our presence, whereas it is safe to say that most if not all the students will at least pretend to complete the task. Another factor that influences our chances of success is the topic of research. Controversial topics are more likely to attract respondents than bland topics, up to a point. In our news media–rich world, the public soon tires of the often excessive news coverage of particular stories. Despite all the possible scenarios under which researchers may attempt to gather data, we have a few recommendations and suggestions that are likely to enhance the chances of success for researchers for whom every data point in a small sample is extremely valuable.

In response to the question of instrument length, let us say that consideration must be given to make instruments *neither too long nor too short*. For instance, the Federal Office of Management and Budget, which we assume has conducted a fair number of surveys, sets guidelines for its surveys to last no longer than thirty minutes (Fowler, 1993, p. 103). We believe that a reasonable duration for the administration (self or otherwise) of an instrument is between fifteen and twenty minutes, a number derived from experience doing this type of research.

Obviously, instruments must be clearly and legibly reproduced and organized in such a way that the subject can easily follow the instructions. Attention must be given to factors such as font size and style, general layout, and apparent reading difficulty. To a reasonable degree, aesthetic considerations should yield to concerns for clarity and accessibility, either while reading the items or listening to someone read them; distinctively unattractive tests do not elicit productive response behaviors.

Finally, choose a title for your test that, without being misleading, does not precipitate test-taking biases among the subjects that are inaccurate and counterproductive. For instance, Perry's instrument was called "A Survey of Health-Related Opinions"; Metcalf's was called "A Study of Public Opinion"; Martin's, although dealing with a different topic than did Perry's instrument, nevertheless made use of the same title. Instrument titles often do not advertise the researcher's research question in ways that may trigger patterned positions and stereotypical views of self among subjects. The goal ought to be neither to discourage participation nor to encourage response sets such as "I'm going to answer all of these items like the loyal Democrat I am!"

Throughout this guide to constructing your own tests for research purposes, we discuss dichotomous as well as continuous and discontinuous closed response item types. As we have seen, dichotomous items are of the yes/no, true/false, right/wrong type. In contrast, continuous and discontinuous items offer more response options. Examples of continuous response options include fully agree, mildly agree, mildly disagree, fully disagree or completely certain, somewhat more certain than uncertain, somewhat more uncertain than certain, and completely uncertain. Discontinuous response items do not mark points along a continuum. Instead, they offer a set of different responses to the question. Items from the U.S. Census Bureau for race/ethnicity (e.g., white, American Indian or Alaska Native, Asian, black or African American, Native Hawaiian, Other Pacific Islander, and Latino or Hispanic), native language, and occupation are examples of discontinuous items. Both continuous and discontinuous types of items can be used in the same instrument, but care should be taken that each type of item be weighted commensurably in arriving at total scores.

Another important consideration while creating test items is that every instrument has a criterial direction. In other words, every test has a response pattern that yields a higher score on the dimension being measured. If the instrument measures attitudes toward "English Only in Government," a higher criterial score would be indicative of more agreement with this position. If the instrument measures "Successful coping with cancer," then a higher score would be indicative of more successful coping. The same can be said of individual items: Each item also has a more criterial and a less criterial direction of response.

For the most part, it is possible to determine the criterial direction of either individual items or scales or both through an analysis of the subcomponents that make up the dimension that the test measures and their relation to individual items. These subcomponents may or may not include demographic variables. In cases where the particular demographic variable that we are interested in (or approximations thereof) is *not* part of the components revealed through a review of the literature, the criteriality of response may be initially unsettled. Thus, for demographic variables such as birthplace, ethnicity, political preference, and religion, the criteriality of response may initially be somewhat unsettled and may become clear only after preliminary item analysis and before the final revised version of the instrument is administered.

Let us illustrate this using first a dichotomous item and then a four-response alternatives item: Both items are given a maximal weight of 1.00 for the response that agrees most with the external criterion and a response and a weight of 0.00 for the response that is most in disagreement. Dichotomous items are all scored either 1 or 0; continuous items with four alternatives are scored 1, 0.66, 0.33, and 0, respectively.

As noted later, Demographic items also may be either dichotomous or continuous. However, despite their appearance of continuity, demographic items of the latter type often must be coded as collections of individual dichotomous items. For instance, when five religious choices are made available (e.g., Catholic, Protestant, Jew, Other, None), then a respondent who checks off "Catholic" may initially be scored as 1 for that choice and as 0 for each of the other religious choices, until it is entirely clear which (if any) religious identification is associated with the criterial direction of the instrument. Once this is determined, that particular religious identification is either scored +1, if positively related to the criterion, or −1 if the criterial relation is negative, with all other identifications scored 0. However, continuous demographic information, such as age, can be scored into one or another of four or more step intervals (e.g., 1 = ages twenty-five and below; 2 = ages twenty-six to forty-nine; 3 = ages fifty to seventy-four, and 4 = ages seventy-five and above, if age is assumed to be criterial; higher ages should contribute more to total score than younger ages), just like other nondemographic continuous items in the instrument. It is also possible not to include demographic items in the total test score and treat them instead as additional predictors. In that case, the criteriality of response and sign of the demographic items remains to be determined.

Occasionally, the criterial direction of items is not immediately evident. For instance, if we are interested in assessing the role that attitudes toward immigrants among registered voters have on their voting behavior, our review of the literature may suggest to us that casting a ballot may depend more on the strength of the attitude than on its polarity. In other words, voters who feel either very positively or negatively toward immigrants are more likely to cast a vote than those voters who feel indifferent about it, even if the votes are in opposition to each other. Since the criterial direction we are interested in concerns voting (not the nature of the vote), responses associated with both most positive and negative attitudes are scored as 1; lukewarm or indifferent responses are scored 0. An example of such an item is what is known as a *semantic differential scale*, in which two words that are opposite in meaning (e.g., "good" and "bad") anchor the poles of the intervals.[2]

Finally, a word about open-response items or those items that enable respondents to respond in their own words, rather than only to pick among responses provided by the researcher. As a rule, such items are much harder to score. However, if you are willing to invest the considerable extra effort that is needed to score them, they too can be handled as either dichotomous or continuous items. As a rule, open-ended items require the prior construction of a scoring manual and, if available, the prior training of several scorers. The scoring of items as either dichotomous or continuous depends on the response or content options that your scoring manual recognizes. But since working with open-ended items is more difficult, we devote all the intervening chapters to a consideration of closed-item instruments alone.

In the meantime, we close this section with a list of items that Martin, a former student, generated. Table B2.1 shows Martin's initial sixty-four

Table B2.1. Martin's Items and Dimensions for the Medical Coping Instrument, Version 1 (MCI-1)

Dimension I: Proactive Behavorial	Dimension II: Reactive Behavorial
1. Tried new activities	3. Participated in risky/impulsive
10. Try to be with people	activities
11. Pamper self/do favorite things	4. Avoided people
15. Alternative healing practices	6. Watched TV
19. Act in community to aid awareness	9. Take out frustrations on others
23. Engaged in physical exercise	13. Sleep to relieve stress
26. Sought professional	14. Eat to relieve stress
therapy/counseling	21. Keep a stiff upper lip
28. Increased daily work/activity load	30. Kept others from knowing how
29. Socialize more outside the home	bad
32. Write more letters/speak on phone	33. Would like to talk, have no one
35. Express emotions, good and bad	27. Use alcohol, cigarettes to relieve
38. Engaged family and friends	stress
in healing	50. Protect family and others by not
42. Cry to relieve stress	discussing
44. Volunteered in community	51. Depended on others to handle
45. Spent more time with family	things
55. Relieved stress by talking with others	53. Avoid stress by caring for others
58. Effort to enjoy/laugh more	57. Noncompliant with medical
59. Discussed with close	regime
friends/confidante	60. Role in family significantly
64. Joined support group for illness	changed

(continued)

Table B2.1. Martin's Items and Dimensions for the Medical Coping Instrument, Version 1 (MCI-1) (*continued*)

Dimension III: *Proactive Cognitive*	Dimension IV: *Reactive Cognitive*
2. Tried meditation	7. Rely primarily on prayer
5. Write in journal	8. Keep emotions to myself
12. Use relaxation techniques	16. Hope for a miracle
18. Used library to gain information	17. Avoid thinking about it
20. Reprioritized things in life	25. Felt lonely since illness
22. Used visualization techniques	34. Refuse to believe it happened
24. Gain information from others	39. Ignore it and block it out
31. Actively structured attitudes	40. Lack of control of life in general
36. Changed or grew in a positive way	41. Lack energy to fight stress
37. Increased creativity since illness	43. Want to run away from it all
52. More spiritual since illness	46. Unable to control the illness
56. Constructed mental plan of action	47. Often think, "Why me?"
61. Possess a strong fighting spirit	48. Often blame self for illness
62. Think of self as a survivor	49. Not think about difficult things
63. Think that life is worth living	54. Believe more in fate

items (along four different subdimensions) for the first draft of her Medical Coping Index. We will return to them later in the next chapter, to see how both the items and the subdimensions fared as a result of item analysis.

Doing a Dry Run: Pilot-Testing the First Version

Nothing is ever as simple as it should be or as we think it will be. Most tests for research purposes will normally *not* be administered to people just like us (the test constructors). The respondents are likely to include a variety of people quite different from those with whom the test constructor may be accustomed to communicate. Consequently, it is not ever possible to fully predict all the things that can go wrong once the collection of data actually begins. A good—albeit pessimistic—adage to keep in mind is this: In the beginning, anything that can go wrong will go wrong.

To anticipate a few more of these possibly minor (but also possibly major) catastrophes, faux pas, snafus, or just plain tough breaks and oversights, it is highly desirable to do a dry run. The subjects included in a dry run ought to be as similar to the target audience as possible; they must also be unlikely to leak word of the nature, purpose, or content of the test back to the remaining pool of subjects. It is best to get possibly negative reactions to the intended instrument *before* fully committing to using a test; better, indeed, than to get such reactions when the instrument is being put to full-scale use. Although the dry run administration should use the same administration routine that is being planned in conjunction with the final administration of the instrument, *it should then be followed up by a serious explorative discussion probing the reactions of each individual subject.* At this point in test development, it is not only appropriate but desirable to organize discussion groups among subjects about specific issues related to the test and the phenomenon it aims to study.

After the instrument's try-out administration, some of these dry-run subjects should be given another copy of the form they have just completed and asked questions that might help in revising the form. Researchers should try to find out what the dry-run subjects liked or disliked about the instrument. We offer the following questions as guidance:

1. What did they think about the amount of time that it took to complete it?
2. Were any of the words hard to read or understand?
3. Were any of the questions ambiguous or unclear?
4. Was the layout crowded?
5. Was the typeface large enough?
6. What about the instructions?
7. Did the subjects feel they were able to express their real opinions, beliefs, or preferences?
8. What dimension of human behavior did they think the instrument tapped?
9. Are there any other questions that the subjects think they should have been asked in order for researchers to better understand the dimension actually being studied?
10. When a random few questions are gone over with individual subjects privately, do they seem to understand what the questions are asking?
11. Can they explain why they selected the responses that they had indicated in their replies?

Investigators are often amazed at the help that the dry run provides. It may seem like such a minor precaution to take, but even when we do not have any serious doubts as to whether we should do one thing or another, according to some of the examples cited later, it is nevertheless well worth the extra time that it requires. This is also the case even when the researchers are quite experienced hands at instrument construction for research purposes.

At the same time, we need to sound a word of caution regarding the interpretation of the informants' responses during the debriefing sessions to follow a dry run. One must be cautious about items that tend to generate too much response agreement among the informants, since such items are likely, subsequently, to yield too little response variance. Similarly, be suspicious of excessively positive reactions among informants. Although answering a series of questions need not be a grueling chore, it cannot be a mindless exercise, either. Typically, items that encourage subjects to rush in their answers do not engage them deeply enough for their responses to be particularly meaningful. As with the findings of each of the item analysis procedures that follow, the decision as to whether to keep, modify, or discard each initial item must be made only after careful evaluation of all the dry run information.

Let us explore specific dry-run concerns using our former students' work as examples. Metcalf wondered whether administering some forms by reading them to subjects who might have reading difficulties would produce different reactions than asking subjects to complete the instrument on their own. He relied on a dry run to find out whether there would be differences between the two ways to administer the test, before attempting a first-run administration. He detected no particular differences between the self- and the researcher-administered conditions as far as comments, reactions, and interpretations of his subjects were concerned. Nevertheless, he decided to also pursue this question at the data analysis stage—when he again utilized both types of administrations—because differences might well crop up *there* rather than around instrument understandability. Another student, Kahn, who was administering some forms via American Sign Language and others via regular aural-oral administration, investigated a similarly serious question. After analyzing the response data, he concluded that there were no significant differences between the two modes of response.

Some researchers may want to be sure whether subjects who are ill or upset can, nevertheless, reply meaningfully to the questions that have been formulated. Others may wonder whether the lay public can understand certain technical vocabulary or whether such vocabulary should be avoided altogether. A common concern is whether the level of grammatical complexity used (e.g., double negatives, embedded clauses) is or is not problematic for the educational level of the intended subjects. Institutionalized subjects may be hostile, spiteful, or uninterested or turned off to the idea of participating in an investigation. Thus, they may fail to answer many items or answer entire blocks of items randomly or ridiculously. An even more common concern is to find out how long the administration per se takes. Indeed, this information is usually needed when requesting permission from administrators (e.g., directors, attending physicians, superintendents, department chairs, teachers) or even from subjects who often have to approve our requests to administer the forms that we have prepared. These are all issues, questions, and concerns for which it would be helpful to have some form of reassurance about the time required before going into the field with a full-blown data collection effort.

For the dry run to serve researchers in any or all these alerting and sensitizing respects, it is necessary that the subjects not be informed initially that what is being brought to their attention is not the final instrument. Quite the contrary, the subjects should be maximally representative of the universe in which researchers are really interested. Furthermore, subjects should understand that the researchers are interested in their responses—which is true, after all. Therefore, the entire dry-run testing experience should be as close as possible in time of day, rapport between researchers and subjects, time pressures under which all concerned, operating, lighting, heating, and noise conditions, among others, to the conditions that are likely during the actual data collection phase. However, en toto dry-run administrations must take more than the usual time per subject because all first drafts are purposely longer than the final versions turn out to be. (More about that in the next chapter.) Furthermore, subjects are then questioned about their reactions, responses, feelings, and beliefs in ways that will not be necessary when the finished instrument is finally used.

The maxim of the dry run should be "better safe than sorry." Even if one finds out some disturbing things—including that opposition to one's research is rife among the very subjects that one has to study, or that one's sponsorship lacks the prestige needed to maximize subject participation, or that one's intended instrument is quite inadequate or seriously problematic in one way or another, among other possibilities—it is far better to find them out sooner rather than later and on a smaller rather than a larger scale. The dry run is a major way in which researchers are alerted to the dangers, misunderstandings, and miscalculations that plague all human interaction and that therefore, to a greater or lesser degree, inevitably visit the research process and its instruments as well.

Should five-point or seven-point response options be used? Should sensitive demographics be probed? Is "altruistic behavior" an expression that only college students understand? Is a Spanish version needed for public relations or linguistic reasons, or for both? The dry run is a chance to answer these and other related questions that worry the test constructor before serious trouble strikes.

Notes

1. These represent questions that former students have come up with while developing their tests and that we now have our current students consider as they draft their own first versions.

2. Semantic differential scales are particularly suitable to measure subjects' feelings toward a particular attitude object, especially when the attitude does not include a well-thought-out position. We refer readers interested in learning more about this type of scales to Snider and Osgood's (1969) *Semantic Differential Technique*.

~

Analyzing Version 1: Item Statistics and Instrument Reliability

The time to evaluate and act on the item characteristics of version 1 is now at hand. The evaluation procedure consists of first obtaining difficulty, consistency, and discriminability scores for each item, in that order. These scores are then used together to decide on each item's ultimate fate. As mentioned in chapter A5, it is only after careful consideration of all these item characteristics, including observations made while pilot-testing the instrument, that a reasonable decision may be reached for each item.

We begin by evaluating item difficulty for various reasons. First, item difficulty is a notion that is familiar to most anyone who has ever had to take a test. Second, the need to code each item according to the direction of criteriality offers an opportunity to assess the subcomponentiality of the instrument and, by implication, its construct validity. Finally, analyzing the distribution of the items' difficulty scores helps us avoid overly skewed distributions indicative of either ceilings or floors in the scores. We ought to note, however, that a normal distribution is no guarantee of a sound instrument, since such distribution of difficulty scores may be due to random responses by the informants. Furthermore, in developing the best test possible for research purposes, we must work toward building desirable levels of item consistency and, eventually, discriminability. The goal is to assemble a set of items that (1) elicit scores with useful variance, (2) contribute to the overall reliability of the instrument, and (3) agree with the total test score without any one item being almost equivalent to it. We must remember to strive toward item discriminability scores that are both above acceptable levels and normally distributed.

After analyzing the items individually, it is necessary to assess the reliability of the entire instrument in order to have a baseline for comparison with subsequent test versions. We should also remind the reader that, though all of these estimates of reliability at either the item or instrument level are essentially correlational in nature, in fact, different procedures are used to estimate the various forms of reliability. An elaboration on these and related theoretical topics that inform the approach to item analyses that we describe can be found in chapter A5. Similarly, we recommend that the reader review chapter A3 on instrument reliability.

Item Analyses

Let us now begin the actual item analyses by following Perry's data, to see how that student-researcher reacted to the results initially obtained on a "Fear of Cancer Self-Screening" instrument. Perry's item distributions were shown in chapter A5 (figures A5.1, A5.4, and A5.6) and need not be reproduced here. What were Perry's reactions to her version 1 results at the item level? We need to remember that the scale represents the items' criteriality. Hence, "difficult" items are those with low criteriality scores.[1] As shown in figure A5.1, Perry's analysis revealed an undesirable buildup of six items at the low scale end of the item difficulty distribution. If these "excessively difficult" items were to be eliminated, the difficulty distribution as a whole would probably be improved in a readministration of the instrument, and its mean difficulty would probably decrease somewhat.

Let us follow these six items a little further by also examining their interitem consistency status (figure A5.4). This graph also shows an excessively long tail and even a miniclustering of items that are clearly less desirable; they have very low median interitem correlations.

Of the six items that seemed most clearly expendable concerning their *difficulty* (items 16, 8, 7, 19, 26, and 15), all but the last mentioned are also poor performers regarding *median interitem consistency*. However, this item (15), poor though it is in item difficulty, turns out to be a very desirable item from the point of view of interitem consistency. Similarly, some of the poorest items insofar as interitem consistency is concerned are quite good items with respect to difficulty (e.g., items 22, 23, and even 13).

The lack of full agreement between item status on the separate dimensions that we have just examined is further illustrated when we look at the third dimension: item discriminability (figure A5.6). However, median interitem consistency and item discriminability scores are, overall, in greater agreement with each other than are either of them with item difficulty scores. Such an agreement between consistency and discriminability scores is to be expected since validity presupposes reliability. Nevertheless, judging thirty items on each of three item analysis dimensions is difficult because items can appear desirable on one dimension and less desirable on another. We have found that compiling the scores for all three dimensions of item analysis facilitates the decision process.

Table B3.1 represents the decision sheet that Perry employed in building an improved version 2 of her "Fear of Cancer Self-Screening" test, based on the item information obtained from version 1. Being rather

Table B3.1. Perry's Decision Sheet for the Fear of Cancer Self-Screening Instrument, Version 1 (FCSSI-1)

Item	Dimension	Difficulty	Consistency	Discriminability	Decision
1	KNOW1	3.8	0.24	0.32	Drop
2	KNOW2	3.4	0.32	0.41	Rewrite
6	KNOW3	3.6	0.38	0.67	Drop
9	KNOW4	2.9	0.43	0.78	Drop
10	KNOW5	4.0	0.47	0.75	Drop
17	KNOW6	3.1	0.38	0.67	Keep
21	KNOW7	3.8	0.44	0.63	Keep
23	KNOW8	3.6	0.08	0.11	Drop
28	KNOW9	3.0	0.50	0.68	Keep
29	KNOW10	3.5	0.44	0.82	Rewrite
3	SERI1	4.4	0.27	0.47	Keep
11	SERI2	4.5	0.40	0.61	Drop
18	SERI3	4.9	0.37	0.59	Keep
25	SERI4	4.9	0.34	0.60	Keep
27	SERI5	3.5	0.43	0.57	Drop
4	VUL1	3.2	0.44	0.79	Rewrite
12	VUL2	3.3	0.25	0.53	Drop
15	VUL3	2.2	0.42	0.72	Drop
22	VUL4	5.3	0.04	0.09	Rewrite
24	VUL5	2.5	0.31	0.50	Keep
26	VUL6	2.3	0.21	0.39	Drop
30	VUL7	3.1	0.37	0.67	Keep
5	PAIN1	2.7	0.19	0.30	Rewrite
13	PAIN2	3.0	0.17	0.31	Rewrite
19	PAIN3	2.1	0.19	0.34	Drop
7	COG1	2.3	0.25	0.37	Drop
14	COG2	3.9	0.40	0.65	Keep
20	COG3	2.4	0.12	0.29	Drop
8	DANG1	2.2	0.22	0.45	Drop
16	DANG2	2.2	0.24	0.44	Drop

tough minded, Perry decided to drop fifteen of her initial thirteen items and to rewrite six others. Only nine of the original thirty items came through the first item analysis unscathed. Indeed, Perry chose to remove entirely the "Perceived Danger" subdimension of the instrument. In addition to the item analyses results, she relied on theoretical considerations in reaching her decision. Similarly, she decided to keep only one item out of the original three for the "Cognitive" subdimension and rewrite two out of three items (numbers 5 and 13) from the "Pain Expectation" subdimension, with the hope of improving their performance in the evaluation of version 2 of the test. Fortunately, Perry had enough items on each of her other three subdimensions (Knowledge, Perceived Seriousness, and Vulnerability) so that at least half of them endured the high standards that Perry imposed upon them.

But what if it had *not* been theoretically and practically acceptable to Perry to jettison the "Perceived Danger" subdimension? In that case, she would have had to design a new set of corresponding items and test a second version with an entire subdimension completely lacking item analysis data, a most undesirable situation. There is no way in which to avoid such a difficult scenario completely, but substantial protection can be assured by starting out with more than enough items on each subdimension. In that way, even with considerable attrition, there is a much better chance that each subdimension will weather the rigors of version 1 item analysis.

So, how many items per subdimension are enough? This is a familiar question for which the answer "The more, the better" should not be surprising. In practical terms, this translates to the following rule of thumb: at least fifteen items per version 1 subdimension. Turning now to table B3.2, we note Martin's decision sheet for version 1 of her "Medical Coping Instrument" (MCI-1). The values on this decision sheet are a compilation of those on figures A5.2, A5.3, and A5.5. Keeping in mind that her interitem consistency score is actually an alpha-if-item deleted score rather than the more desirable median, or even the mean interitem correlation score, we may note that the outcome was somewhat similar to that in Perry's case. Of the original sixty-four items, Martin decided to retain only forty without any changes. She also chose to rewrite two items and add four new items. She based the latter on the same substantive content that was covered by the equivalent number of omitted items. Even though the overall attrition rate for Martin's items was less than that for Perry's items, she opted to combine two subdimensions, "Reactive-Behavioral" and "Reactive-Cognitive," into a single "Reactive-Coping" subdimension (see tables B3.2 and B3.3). As with Perry, Martin based her decision on both the item analysis results

Table B3.2. Martin's Decision Sheet for Medical Coping Instrument, Version 1 (MCI-1)

Item	Dimension	Difficulty	Consistency	Discriminability	Decision
1	1	3.00	0.793	0.351	Keep
2	2	2.00	0.792	0.362	Keep
3	3	4.45	0.799	0.095	Rewrite
4	3	4.18	0.800	0.040	Drop
5	2	1.40	0.799	0.091	Drop
6	3	3.68	0.790	0.429	Keep
7	4	3.13	0.812	−0.247	Drop
8	4	3.68	0.788	0.536	Keep
9	3	4.23	0.801	0.007	Drop
10	1	3.36	0.796	0.235	Keep
11	1	3.00	0.802	−0.015	Drop
12	2	2.23	0.786	0.597	Keep
13	3	3.73	0.803	−0.100	Drop
14	3	3.82	0.801	0.066	Keep
15	1	1.95	0.798	0.157	Keep
16	4	3.82	0.808	−0.129	Drop
17	4	3.77	0.789	0.501	Keep
18	2	3.00	0.805	−0.080	Drop
19	1	2.09	0.795	0.271	Keep
20	2	3.86	0.788	0.603	Keep
21	3	3.59	0.783	0.631	Keep
22	2	2.14	0.795	0.261	Keep
23	1	3.41	0.796	0.233	Keep
24	2	4.32	0.794	0.435	Keep
25	4	4.00	0.805	−0.159	Drop
26	1	2.55	0.803	0.021	Drop
27	3	4.73	0.797	0.226	Drop/rewrite
28	1	2.32	0.805	−0.126	Drop
29	1	3.23	0.793	0.394	Keep
30	3	4.18	0.799	0.095	Keep
31	2	3.36	0.793	0.325	Keep
32	1	2.86	0.794	0.303	Keep
33	3	4.45	0.800	0.033	Drop/replace
34	4	4.55	0.798	0.181	Drop
35	1	3.14	0.792	0.429	Keep
36	2	3.86	0.785	0.731	Keep
37	2	3.23	0.790	0.731	Keep
38	1	3.27	0.786	0.528	Keep
39	4	4.31	0.792	0.471	Keep
40	4	3.59	0.810	−0.303	Drop
41	4	3.95	0.808	−0.239	Drop
42	1	2.27	0.798	0.149	Keep
43	4	3.54	0.795	0.299	Keep
44	1	3.32	0.794	0.313	Keep

(*continued*)

Table B3.2. Martin's Decision Sheet for Medical Coping Instrument, Version 1 (MCI-1) (*continued*)

Item	Dimension	Difficulty	Consistency	Discriminability	Decision
45	1	3.18	0.791	0.390	Keep
46	4	3.86	0.800	0.064	Drop
47	4	4.05	0.794	0.359	Keep
48	4	4.77	0.797	0.227	Drop
49	4	4.09	0.800	0.054	Drop
50	3	4.00	0.797	0.229	Keep
51	3	4.50	0.798	0.161	Keep
52	2	3.00	0.794	0.300	Keep
53	3	3.36	0.810	−0.278	Drop/replace
54	4	3.55	0.807	−0.085	Drop
55	1	3.27	0.791	0.400	Keep
56	2	2.64	0.782	0.653	Keep
57	3	4.45	0.804	−0.103	Drop
58	1	3.68	0.794	0.340	Keep
59	1	3.50	0.790	0.443	Keep
60	3	3.77	0.809	−0.263	Drop
61	2	3.82	0.788	0.543	Keep
62	2	4.59	0.789	0.646	Drop
63	2	4.45	0.791	0.463	Keep
64	1	4.13	0.795	0.267	Keep

for version 1 of her test *and* a consideration of the conceptual framework behind the subdimensions.

In both cases, the issue must now be raised as to the effect of the resulting lack of proportion between subdimensions when some that were initially proposed are either dropped entirely or combined. Obviously, the new total score taps something somewhat different, when some subdimensions are measured by many more items than others. Similarly, a subdimension dropped or amalgamated with another has very definite implications for what the total score means or represents vis-à-vis the construct or underlying behavioral phenomenon that the test is measuring. This is not a measurement issue alone; it is an issue that has definite consequences for both conceptual and empirical validity. When version 2 of a test is substantially differently designed or redesigned due to item analysis results, the validity criterion to be employed must be carefully rethought as well. Does the originally selected criterion still appear to be as appropriate for the revised instrument as it was thought to be originally? Is it still desirable for this criterion to be the final arbiter of the "goodness" or fidelity of the test, as it appeared to be when the test was initially being designed? If not, then

Table B3.3.   Items and Dimensions of Martin's Medical Coping Instrument, Version 2 (MCI-2)

Dimension I: Proactive Behavioral	Dimension II: Proactive Cognitive	Dimension III: Reactive Coping
1. Have undertaken new activities/hobbies	2. Used meditation	3. Watched TV to distract myself
5. Made an effort to be around others	6. Used relaxation	4. Kept emotions/stress to myself
10. Acted in community funding	8. Researched/tried alternative healing	7. Tried to feel better by eating
14. Engaged in program of exercise	11. Reprioritized important things	9. Avoided thinking about illness
15. Communicated with others/information	13. Used visualizations	12. Maintained a "stiff upper lip"
17. Socialized as much as possible	19. Restructured attitudes toward illness and life	16. Tried to feel better through substances (smoking, drinking)
20. Wrote letters/made telephone calls	22. Changed or grew in positive way	18. Kept important people from knowing how bad it is
21. Expressed aloud emotions	23. Acted or thought creatively	
24. Engaged family/friends in healing	33. Became more spiritual	25. Ignored the whole situation
26. Cried	35. Constructed mental plan of action	27. Felt like I wanted to run away from it all
28. Volunteered in community	38. Developed strong fighting spirit	30. Pondered, "Why me?"
29. Spent more time with family	42. Sought or considered psychological counseling	31. Protected family by not discussing condition
34. Relieved stress by talking it over	43. Felt I can count on someone for emotional support	32. Depended mostly on others to handle things
36. Made an effort to enjoy/laugh more	44. Devoted more energy taking care of myself	39. Felt helpless
37. Discussed inner feelings	45. Maintained feeling that life is worth living	40. Devoted more energy to taking care of others
46. Participated in support group		41. Been more risky/impulsive in behaviors

now is the time to rethink the validity criterion and to pick a more appropriate one, if such can be found, based on the test's new emphases or subcomponential balance.

Instrument Reliability

The computer statistical packages (e.g., SPSS) that calculate the item statistics for version 1 also offer the researcher an opportunity to obtain the instrument's overall reliability score. Perry's version 1 of her "Fear of Cancer Self-Screening Test" produced an instrument alpha score of 0.90; Martin's version 1 of her "Medical Coping Instrument," an instrument alpha of 0.80. Both of these values were certainly high enough as indicators of measurement stability at the instrument level to warrant going ahead with constructing, administering, and analyzing a version 2 for each one.

Will there be a noticeable improvement between the first and second versions for all the item and instrument indicators of relevance? Or, as Galton discovered in his investigation of height in humans, will they be overcome by regression toward the mean? This is a particularly likely trend when working with the small samples that our readers will usually obtain. And finally, the superquestion of them all: What validity will they be able to demonstrate? The latter is the question on which all further plans to utilize researcher constructed tests for subsequent investigative purposes necessarily hinges.

Before we leave this chapter, we ought to expand somewhat on the notion behind the term *regression toward the mean*. Physical scientists are fortunate in that, other than small measurement errors, technological advances have helped reduce considerably; what they see is what they get. In contrast, social scientists must always contend with the fact that social phenomena are less transparent, less constant, less controllable, and usually involve several variables that relate with each other in complex ways. No matter how careful we are in thinking about, drafting, and field-testing an instrument, we cannot be certain that every new subject will interpret every item in the manner that previous subjects have or even in the same manner in future occasions. Indeed, it is possible that a particular subject holds a particular bias against a word in an item that taints her response. Or she may be distracted by any one of a host of possible occurrences competing for her attention. Or she may feel particularly upbeat because she just received a salary increase, and her mood colors her response to an item asking her about her attitudes toward the homeless. Furthermore, it is almost certain that none of these conditions would be the same were our subject to respond to the item again, even if she had no memory of having done so. Were we to administer the same item to the same subject in repeated occasions, her scores would cluster around a mean score. Were we to wager on her response, it would be precisely this mean score that we would bet on, and not the few very high or low scores she obtained most recently. The tendency of extreme or atypical scores not to reoccur is what *regression toward the mean* refers to.

When working with large samples, extreme scores tend to have less of an impact on research results. The same cannot be said of small samples such as those most researchers using this book will rely on. First, the impact of extreme scores is magnified in small samples. Second, such scores are the least likely to reoccur. And third, since it is a product moment coefficient, extreme scores disproportionately influence the correlation coefficient. For this reason, when extreme scores do not reoccur (because they are the least likely to occur in the first place), all the measures that they describe appear to be less favorable than what we expected. Still, a silver lining of sorts exists regarding regression toward the mean. Because of it, we may obtain poorer instrument reliability scores than we hoped for. However discouraging this may seem to beginning researchers, they must remember that a pessimistic estimate of reliability offers added protection against false positives even if increasing the probability of a false negative, a pattern that agrees with widely accepted scientific norms and values.

Note

1. All items must have the same number of response options in order to carry out the various item analyses. Thus, differences in response options (e.g., yes/no, high/medium/low, fully agree/agree somewhat/disagree somewhat/fully disagree) must be recoded to equivalent values to avoid erroneous results.

~

Analyzing Version 2: Item Statistics, Instrument Reliability, and Validity

Having completed all the improvements suggested by the item analyses described in the previous chapter, it is time to evaluate version 2 of the test. The process is essentially the same as that used to evaluate version 1, with the exception that this time we will test for the test's *criterion validity*. It is worth noting that the procedure we have discussed so far (i.e., assessment of item difficulty, consistency, and discriminability, followed by an estimation of the instrument's reliability, resulting in item changes) may be repeated as many times as deemed necessary. We realize, however, that beginning researchers may be hard-pressed to apply this method more than three times because of limited time and other resources. Thus, we see the need to carefully evaluate each item using as much information about it as possible. However painstakingly laborious the procedure may seem to researchers facing real and immediate deadlines, the benefits of assembling a reliable and valid test are long-lasting and worthy of the effort.

Item Statistics and Instrument Reliability

Version 2 reveals whether all the work and hopes connected with version 1 have paid off. After careful selection and preliminary testing of items, further refining of these items based on empirical evidence, it is time to address the issue of instrument validity. Sometimes, however, the best-laid plans of mice and men do not pan out as hoped or, as it happens more often than not in test construction for research purposes, do not pan out completely. If that is the case, researchers ought to consider repeating the cycle again to develop a version 3 of the test.

The fact is that there is no magic hidden reason behind suggesting that a test should undergo at least two trials before it is used for research. So long as the refinement process reflects a cyclical interaction between theory and empirical evidence, and barring catastrophic (and improbable) regression toward the mean effects, a test can only improve with further trials and refinements. At some point, however, the improvements become almost negligible in comparison to the effort invested, which certainly ought to be of concern to beginning researchers with minimal resources. Let us see, first, how Martin fared on the analyses of results stemming from the second trial of her "Medical Coping Index" test. We will then turn to some other illustrative results as well.

As the data reveal, the revisions that Martin carried out toward a version 2 of her instrument resulted in improvements over her version 1. The mean item difficulty score (figure B4.1) increased somewhat, approaching the midpoint of the possible response range, and the distribution curve for the main body of the obtained responses is approximately bell shaped. There is, of course, a worrisome cluster of items with anti-criterial responses. These would be a prime target for further revision or maybe even deletion, if a version 3 were ultimately judged to be in order.

The interitem consistency picture is also somewhat improved (figure B4.2), rising ever so slightly from a former mean of 0.799 to a new mean of 0.801. The shape of the curve is nothing to crow about (although neither was its shape in version 1), but this flattening and the abbreviated range of values obtained are a direct consequence of Martin's use of the alpha-if-item-deleted correlations instead of median or mean interitem correlations, which always show more variance.

Finally, the item discriminability indices in figure B4.3 (expressed as "Corrected Item-Total Correlation") also show a somewhat improved mean, rising from 0.215 to 0.265. As before, this is a very low mean and implies, even after any correction for rough-grouping due to the use of Pearsonian correlations, that there may be items, or even subscales, that are working against the total score and that should be either deleted or developed into separate instruments. Again, the shape of the distribution is flat, which leads to the same conclusion—namely, that a third version and further dimensional refinement of the "Medical Coping Index" test might be not only possible but also necessary.

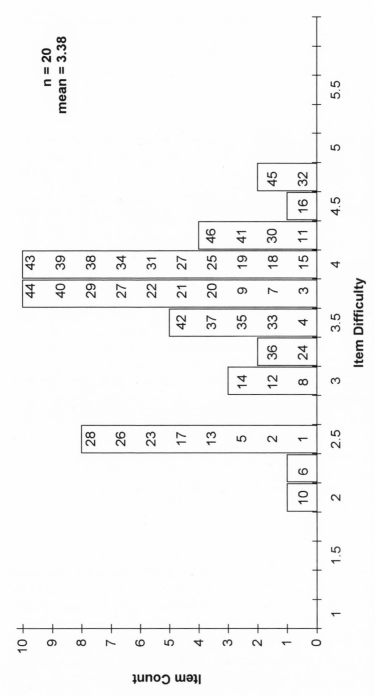

Figure B4.1. Martin's Item Difficulty Scores Distribution for the Medical Coping Instrument, Version 2 (MCI-2)

Note: Numbers in bars are item numbers.

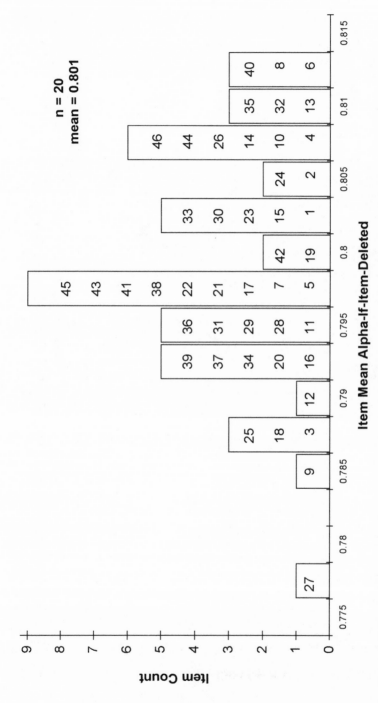

Figure B4.2. Martin's Item Consistency Scores Distribution (Alpha-if-Item-Deleted) for Medical Coping Index, Version 2 (MCI-2)

Note: Numbers in bars are item numbers.

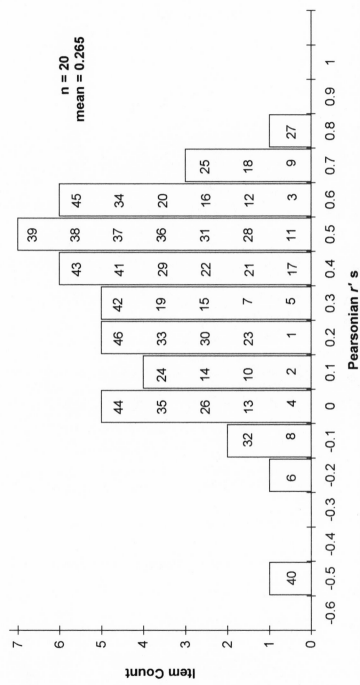

Figure B4.3. Item Discriminability Scores (Corrected Item–Total Pearsonian Correlations) for Martin's Medical Coping Index, Version 2 (MCI-2)

Note: Numbers in bars are item numbers.

Table B4.1. Decision Sheet for Martin's Medical Coping Instrument, Version 2 (MCI-2)

Item	Dimension	Difficulty	Consistency	Discriminability	Decision
1	1	2.45	0.802	0.154	Keep
2	2	2.40	0.804	0.094	Revise & merge
3	3	3.60	0.787	0.532	Keep
4	3	3.25	0.806	−0.004	Drop
5	1	2.35	0.797	0.293	Keep
6	2	2.20	0.815	−0.296	Revise & merge
7	3	3.70	0.797	0.292	Keep
8	2	2.85	0.812	−0.134	Drop
9	3	3.60	0.783	0.669	Keep
10	1	1.95	0.805	0.027	Keep
11	2	4.02	0.794	0.478	Keep
12	3	2.95	0.789	0.539	Keep
13	2	2.35	0.809	−0.059	Revise & merge
14	1	2.80	0.805	0.010	Keep
15	1	3.80	0.800	0.215	Keep
16	3	4.25	0.791	0.570	Keep
17	1	2.35	0.795	0.365	Keep
18	3	3.80	0.785	0.651	Keep
19	2	3.80	0.798	0.256	Keep
20	1	3.70	0.790	0.570	Keep
21	1	3.70	0.795	0.370	Keep
22	2	3.65	0.796	0.350	Keep
23	2	2.30	0.801	0.168	Keep
24	1	3.15	0.804	0.059	Keep
25	3	3.90	0.786	0.642	Keep
26	1	2.35	0.806	−0.077	Drop
27	3	3.95	0.777	0.901	Keep
28	1	2.25	0.794	0.434	Keep
29	1	3.65	0.794	0.367	Keep
30	3	4.05	0.802	0.118	Keep
31	3	3.70	0.793	0.444	Keep
32	3	4.50	0.808	−0.154	Drop
33	2	3.35	0.802	0.111	Keep
34	1	3.75	0.791	0.562	Keep
35	2	3.30	0.808	−0.009	Drop
36	1	3.20	0.793	0.407	Keep
37	1	3.40	0.792	0.429	Keep
38	2	3.85	0.795	0.482	Keep
39	3	3.85	0.792	0.500	Keep
40	3	3.50	0.822	−0.508	Revise & recode
41	3	4.10	0.797	0.326	Keep
42	2	3.45	0.799	0.229	Keep
43	2	3.80	0.796	0.333	Keep
44	2	3.60	0.807	−0.083	Revise & merge
45	2	4.50	0.795	0.501	Keep
46	1	4.10	0.805	0.102	Keep

Another thing that becomes clear from comparing the item statistics from version 1 with those from version 2 (note that some of the item numbers have changed) is that some items jump around considerably in their performance on one item analysis index or another from one version to the next. This is a direct result of working with small and predominantly nonrandom samples. Yet, it is usually not within the time or financial limits of unsupported student-researchers to overcome these limitations. *The best that can be done is to make the most rational decisions possible on the bases of the data that one has collected.* Table B4.1, Martin's decision sheet based on version 2, indicates that were there to be a version 3, ten of the forty-six items in version 2 would be eliminated in one way or another. Finally, we should note that the instrument alpha for version 2 was 0.815—not a bad result at all, considering that version 2 is shorter (forty-six items) than version 1 (sixty-four items) and that version 2's alpha was 0.799.

Criterion Validity

For her validity design, Martin did not use the two-group, two-test paradigm; she used a one-group, three-test paradigm. The revised Medical Coping Index (MCI II) was administered to a single sample, all of whom also replied to the "Coping Scale" developed and tested by Billings and Moos (1981) and the "Generalized Contentment Scale" (GCS) by Hudson (1982). The latter was used as the criterion variable and the former, together with Martin's own MCI II, and various demographics (age, sex, education, marital status, number of children, months since diagnosis, ethnicity, and religion) were all considered as predictor variables. The unforced forward selection procedure results are shown just below the middle of table A5.1.

As can be seen, the optimal predictor of GCS scores was the MCI II. The correlation between these two[1] was 0.576. The next best predictor of GCS, the Billings and Moos (1981) "Coping Scale," provided incremental validity by boosting the overall multiple correlation to 0.695. None of the demographics made any additional contributions to incremental validity. Yet, the two tests *taken together*, accounted for nearly 50 percent of the total variance in the criterion, a value that is much higher than either one of them alone could attain. This is not a bad claim to fame for a researcher-designed test! It turned out to be a better predictor of the criterion selected than an already available, validated, and recognized instrument, even though the previously available instrument still added significantly to the variance accounted for in the criterion, above and beyond what would have been attained without it.

Depending on the prior status of the Billings and Moos (1981) "Coping Scale," Martin may have demonstrated very promising criterion validity and incremental validity for the MCI II. Even better results might be obtained were a version 3 to be prepared. Clearly, it is easier to improve on the performance of a substandard test than on a sound one. The superiority of the researcher's new instrument and even its contributions to incremental validity are all functions of the psychometric soundness of the prior instrument. It is also important to recognize that the conceptual appropriateness of the components vis-à-vis the criterion is at the core of these findings. In chapter A2,we stated the need to consider the internal validity of the test as a point of departure when developing tests for research purposes. As such, we assume that the researcher has a solid understanding of the relevant research literature and that this knowledge has informed the overall choice of constructs and, in Martin's case, existing scales to incorporate into the test. Similarly, an understanding of the theory behind the phenomenon in question informs decisions concerning the removal, change, or retention of individual items.

Attention to building incremental validity at all costs without concern for theory can lead the imprudent researcher to a situation in which a significant degree of criterion variance is accounted for by the variance in test scores, yet it is not clear why this is so. Unless one is careful to go back and forth between theory and the empirical results from each item and instrument analyses, it is difficult to determine what one found out through one's test. This is yet another reason for the need to keep a log in which one keeps track of the item analyses results vis-à-vis theory. It is important to remember that, after all, the reason for our time and efforts is to develop an instrument that will help us explain a phenomenon. Our task is *not* simply to create an instrument that has all the "right" numbers.

Therefore, the decision of whether to take the time needed to develop a version 3 of a test for research purposes depends on both theoretical and practical considerations as well as on the investigator's ultimate research or applied purposes. Certainly, if operational program purposes, such as patients' admission and treatment, were among the potential uses for the MCI II, it would be essential to obtain a much higher validity coefficient. As is, even with the Billings and Moos (1981) "Coping Scale" included, the MCI II only accounts for approximately one-half of the criterion variance. Furthermore, other criteria should be examined as well, before any conclusion is arrived at concerning the adequacy of the validity of the MCI II. Specifically, the validity of a test is only as good as the appropriateness of the criterion it is used to predict. As far as the applied potential of the test is concerned, it would be good if the MCI II could predict a more difficult and costly criterion, rather than merely a score on another easily administered test. In contrast and as far as nonoperational research purposes are concerned, the MCI II may already be a very useful tool, particularly when used in a battery together with other instruments. The very least that should be said for it is that the researcher who created it has done a rather decent job!

The validation approach adopted by Metcalf and colleagues is in some ways similar to and in some ways different from that of Martin. As is common in opinion questionnaire research, the criterion in Metcalf's case was one of the items in the instrument (a "crunch" item): "Are you in favor of or opposed to legislation requiring English only in federal government services?" The purpose of his test construction was to maximally account for variance in the responses to this question. The most valid prior predictor of such responses was an abbreviated (but validated) version of the justly famous "The Implicit Antidemocratic Trends of Potentiality for Fascism Scale" (F-Scale) by Theodor Adorno and colleagues (1993). Metcalf randomly placed six F-Scale items throughout his instrument, which were scored together as a total. In addition, a number of demographic variables were also introduced as predictors. Table B4.2 reports the results that Metcalf obtained.

As in Martin's case, Metcalf's instrument, the English-Only in Government (EOG) Scale contributed to incremental validity. However, that

Table B4.2. Criterion Validity Analysis for Metcalf's English-Only in Government (EOG)

Step	Variable	Cumulative R	Cumulative R^2
1	F score	.410	.168
2	Age	.534	.285
3	Total EOG Attitude Score	.604	.365
4	Political (preference for president; 3/96)	.647	.419
5	Religion (Protestant)	.668	.447
6	Occupation (student)	.682	.465
7	Number of U.S.-born grandparents	.688	.474
8	Sex (male)	.694	.482

is where the similarities end. The prior instrument (the F-Scale, which has been undergoing successive refinement for the past forty years!) remained the best single predictor of the criterion. This finding alone is evidence that the criterion responses were valid and not haphazard, a charge often made about opinion surveys. A simple demographic consideration, age, was the next best predictor. The EOG Scale was the third best predictor, after which five additional demographic considerations continued to boost the multiple significantly until, finally, nearly half of the total variance in the "crunch question" was accounted for.

The great importance of demographic variables in an opinion survey should not be surprising, since the diverse voting age population at large, at least that of the large metropolitan U.S. West Coast area where Metcalf collected his data, was the universe to which generalizations would ultimately be made. This is demographically a far more diversified population and required a larger sample in constructing both version 1 and version 2 of the EOG Scale than is generally the case when constructing most tests for student research purposes. In fact, the decision to include a large sample that was demographically representative of the area's voting population came about after examining what was known regarding voting trends in the population.

As mentioned earlier, demographic variables may have implications for operational tests and their inevitable social policy ramifications that are not found in tests for academic research purposes. In all cases, however, the presence of important demographic variables points to further considerations, beyond the tests themselves that influence criterion performance. For demographers (including sociologists and political scientists), demographic variables are of major interest at their own level of abstraction. In contrast, for psychologists they are primarily indicators of different experiential histories, and, as such, they prompt further exploration of the manifold experiential patterns that contribute either to test or to criterion performance or both. Adachi's results, reported earlier, are also relevant to this discussion in view of the considerable number of demographic variables that he identified in the pursuit of incremental validity.

Yet another former student, Spira, demonstrated another variation in the pursuit of validity. His initial criterion was helplessness, as defined by membership in either the employed or unemployed group. In predicting this group membership criterion, version 2 of his own "Perceived Support Inventory" (PSI-2) came in second to the redoubtable "Beck Hopelessness Scale" (1974), but ahead of the "Family Support Scale" by Dunst and colleagues (1988). The multiple R rose from 0.887 to 0.943 to 0.958 in this approach. Finally, when the "Family Support Scale" was used as criterion, only Spira's PSI-2 was a useful predictor ($R = 0.663$). The "Beck Hopelessness Scale" did not figure at all in the final stepwise regression model. This second finding differentiates Spira's PSI-2 scale from the Beck Hopelessness Scale (the latter being depression related), whereas the first finding combines the two quite effectively in conjunction with a different criterion (Spira's demographically defined helplessness groups).

The results of validity inquiries are the launching pad from which all subsequent research takes off. If the results are deemed adequate, the subsequent steps may involve utilizing the newly created test for empirical research purposes. If, however, the validity-related results are deemed inadequate, it is necessary to return to the drawing board, whether by tackling version 3 or by coming up with a new version 1 along a substantially revised conceptual framework.

Note

1. Although the first step in a multiple correlation is labeled "multiple R," it is really an ordinary zero-order correlation. The two have the same numerical *value*, but the direction of the correlation can be ascertained only from the matrix reporting zero-order correlations (at the top of table B52), since multiple correlations are always positive in sign.

PART B
CHAPTER 5

~

Semiformal Measurement: Varieties of Content Analysis

Formal measurement involves the maximal separation of the measurer from the measurement. If the *measure* is assumed to be an inert vessel, like the alchemists' "test" in olden days, neither causing nor inhibiting the views, attitudes, or abilities that it quantifies, then most certainly the *measurer* also must be distanced to avoid causing any of the results that are obtained. It was this very distancing that distinguished the work of alchemists from that of magicians, who mediated people's perceptions of the real world through their very actions.

Though in this book we view this separation as fundamental to test construction for research purposes, we also recognize that our perspective is by no means the only one. It is not the "right" or "better" one, either. Important philosophical differences exist between our position and one that conceives the researcher as an inextricable part of the phenomenon to be studied. We will not discuss these philosophical differences here. (We refer readers interested in such a discussion to Tashakkori and Teddlie's 1998 book listed among the recommended readings in appendix A.) However, it is true that whether or not researchers view themselves as separate or a part of the phenomenon, researchers interested in test construction often face situations in which it is impossible to be maximally distant from the results of interest.

Phenomena involving subjects who are very young are instances in which a separation between the measurer and the measured is minimal.

At one level, young children lack the literacy skills to be able to complete a research test. Additionally, they may lack the cognitive and linguistic skills to understand and respond appropriately to abstract questions that may not pose much of a challenge for older children. Parents, teachers, doctors, or other specially trained observers who are thoroughly familiar with both the particular behavioral manifestations and with the young subjects that are being studied must, of necessity, respond about those who cannot respond to paper-and-pencil forms themselves. The same may be said for those who are too old or too infirm to give their own responses.

Various human documents such as diaries, therapy protocols, films, radio or TV programs, letters, historical records, among others, require active reading, rating, or interpretation by researchers to be turned into quantitative data for research purposes. However, over and above the examples of subjects who cannot themselves respond to researcher-made measures, some researchers are convinced that *without their personal interaction with the subjects, a vital element is lost*. These researchers believe that the kind of insightful understanding, intuition, and sensitivity that makes the subjects come alive as human beings also enables the researchers to utilize their own subtle sensitivities in order to appropriately formulate the research results. In all of the aforementioned instances, some aspects of formal measurement are still possible. Yet, due to the degree of intervention of the researchers in the data-generating and processing procedures, the results may, at best, be termed semiformal, rather than the kind of formal measurement we have discussed so far.

A Two-Dimensional Grid

Table B5.1 involves two intersecting dichotomous dimensions. Across the top of the table, the dichotomy pertains to (1) whether the presence and involvement of the researcher is necessary in order for the data to come into being or (2) whether the researcher's involvement is required only to score or quantify the data. Along the left-hand margin of table B5.1, the dichotomy pertains to whether (A) content analysis and item analysis are possible or whether (B) only content analysis is possible. Let us now discuss the four cells that result from the intersection of these two dichotomous dimensions.

Table B5.1. Four Kinds of Semiformal Measurement

	Nature of Investigator's Involvement	
Types of Analyses	(1) Generate and Quantify Data	(2) Quantify but Not Generate Data
(A) Content analysis and item analysis	Rating schedules (open or closed)	Biographical inventories (open or closed)
	Interview schedules (open or closed)	Open-ended questions
(B) Only content analysis	Field observations	Prior text analyses –protocols
	Most projective techniques	–diaries and letters –radio programs –films

Intersect 1/B

Let us begin at the bottom of the table and work our way up. Intersect 1/B involves two very prevalent and productive types of nominal level measurement. One type of data consists of Field Observations, including various related field designations and ethnographical participant observation. In all these, *without the presence of the researcher there are no data;* what the researcher records in his or her notes are the data. The researcher's analysis is a report and interpretation of the events that the researcher witnessed and followed personally. The measurer is (or does) the measure, the two being inseparable. The second type of data consists of most Projective Techniques. In this case, we once more depend totally on the researcher to score and interpret the responses that these tests yield. Both the choice of stimulus and interpretation of responses are up to the researcher, a feature that makes this process different from open-ended questionnaires (see the section "Intersect 2/A"). It is worth repeating that, without an individual interpreter who is thoroughly immersed in the data, there are no results.

In both cases, there will be quite different data for different subjects. The data do not consist of items that are identical from one subject to another and that have been set out in advance. The data are whatever a subject has enacted either in the researcher's presence or in response to the test's deliberately ambiguous stimuli. Every respondent to most projective techniques answers his or her own items, responds to whatever stimuli he or she recognizes and prefers. Since there are no uniform arrays of items, in either case, there cannot be comparable total scores to compare across subjects or groups of subjects. Thus, although there is content analysis in both instances by field workers and by clinicians, there is no item analysis as we have come to know it. There is no possibility of setting aside bad items according to their difficulty, consistency, or discriminability because there are no comparable and uniformly established item/response linkages across all of the subjects being studied. Therefore, no aspects of formal measurement are possible in research of this kind.

Intersect 2/B

The situation in this quadrant is similar to the previous quadrant in that there are no prior uniform items. Although these kind of data are not generated in the presence of or by means of the researcher and may actually predate the researcher by any number of years, it still requires a researcher who is completely immersed in the data to discover the topics that the prior texts contain. The topics are derived from the interaction between whatever happens to exist and whatever the researcher happens to recognize. Since there are no preset items, other researchers can examine the same prior texts for entirely different topics.

Content analyses can and must be performed (otherwise, there is no research). Yet, no item analyses are possible, because each researcher recognizes and interprets a different set of possible items, depending on the researcher's particular interests. For instance, one researcher will read Shakespeare to study sex role differences; another will study the same material in order to determine the fluctuating terms of address (formal and informal) that existed in English pronomial usage in the seventeenth century. When a clinical psychologist scores the projective responses that someone else has obtained and does so for a subject whom the scorer does not know at all, then this, too, is a prior text analysis and belongs in this quadrant. The data then are at least quasi-independent of the measurer, although it is clearly less so vis-à-vis the clinician who collected it. Nevertheless, no uniform set of items is available for scoring. Again, this situation precludes the use of formal measurement approaches and, by implication, item analyses.

Intersect 1/A

In this quadrant, we encounter such mainstays of psychological research as rating scales and interview schedules. When the scales and schedules fully enumerate what it is that the researcher should ask and observe (e.g., closed scales, schedules), then these enumerations constitute preestablished items that can be scored and revised by the approaches to item analysis we describe in earlier chapters of this book. An additional example of preestablished items to which it is possible to apply item analyses includes the ratings of films and TV programs based on the amount of adult content (i.e., language, violence, sex) in them. Even if no such preenumerated list is mentioned in the schedules or open scales, it can be superimposed on the observations, interviews, and conversations for scoring purposes. By doing so, items are essentially created, and when no occurrences of certain prespecified behaviors of interest or discourse topics and styles of interest are encountered, then these no-occurrences are scored in the same way as no responses would be scored on a Likert scale.

A common problem that researchers must deal with in general, but especially with rating scales and interview schedules, is that of missing data. The obvious solution is to eliminate items that frequently have been left unanswered. Another possible solution is to fill in the missing data for a given item with a value equal to the total mean score for the entire test. When scales exist, the researcher ought to consider filling in the missing data with the mean response score for that item. This last solution, however, must be approached with caution since it is possible to bring in spurious variance into the item analyses with it. An even more severe approach is to develop either related or separate measures or even tests from those items that are either often rejected by the respondents or that have very low response rates.[1]

Using formal analysis approaches to evaluate rating scales and interview schedules demands the creation of detailed scoring manuals. As with any research instrument or protocol, these scoring manuals must undergo a series of tests and revisions before using them to make sure that every record is coded in the same way and that different raters and interviewers are scoring them in the same way. If there are uniform items, then total scores can be generated and reliability and validity studies can be performed in the usual ways. In essence, this quadrant pursues the maximal formalization of scoring without pursuing the formalization of data collection, since in the latter connection the researcher is fully immersed in the generation of the data of record.

Intersect 2/A

Here we again encounter either open or closed instruments (and the necessarily detailed scoring manuals, which the latter require). However, in contrast with intersect 1/A, the researcher need not be present when the responses to the instruments are generated. The instruments utilized are essentially of the self-response type. Seemingly open-ended-biographical or open-ended-personality questions, such as those that constitute "Rotter's Sentence Completion Test" (Rotter and Rafferty, 1950), are, nevertheless, composed of uniform and specific items. Using a scoring manual, it is possible to score these items and obtain item responses and total scores. In contrast with projective techniques, the role of the researcher is to analyze the data, not choose the items. Indeed, the more closed-ended an instrument is, the more it can also include demographic items as well as randomly scattered items from previously validated instruments. In that case, incremental validity can be explored while perfecting newly developed instruments, some with apparently open response opportunities.

Similarities and Dissimilarities between Formal and Semiformal Measurement

Whether or not the measurer is directly and necessarily involved or enmeshed in the measures that instruments yield is a significant distinction between formal and semiformal measurement. The involvement of the measurer with the measure in intersects 1/A and 1/B is significantly greater than that which is undoubtedly present in the ubiquitous personal factor that permeates all research. Every topic and every method that a researcher selects is, to some extent, a reflection of the researcher's personality and life experience. This is especially true in the social or behavioral sciences.

In semiformal measurement, the researcher creates the scores by performing the interpretations through which content analysis is constituted. It is exactly in order to minimize the bias that derives (or could well derive) from such personal involvement or investment that formal measurement has been implemented and why it pursues the maximal separation between the measure and the measurer. Semiformal measurement is a compromise with this stricture of maximal separation. It is an approach in which one must rely on readers and raters who may be either the researchers themselves or individuals who may be aware of what the research hypotheses are. At the very least, readers and raters may have views of their own as to what is right or wrong, good or bad, in the areas being researched. Still, there is no other way that studies of prior tests can be conducted. As much care as possible needs to be exercised that precise manuals and extensive training of either readers or raters or both will tend to overcome or minimize the biases that constantly endanger such research.

However, the difference between formal and semiformal measurement is most crucially reflected *not* about whether the researcher is maximally distanced from the generation and the quantification of the data. Rather, the crucial difference resides in whether *a uniform set of items is either manifestly or latently present*. Without such a set of items by means of which *every subject is scored on every item, including those left blank* (which is quite a different matter than simply preparing a scoring manual for whatever it is that interests the researcher), no total scores and no item analyses can be obtained. Furthermore, the usual reliability and validity procedures cannot be implemented. We recognize that this may be difficult to accomplish, precisely because manuals are hard to construct, and raters are hard to train, and the problem of interrater agreement requires separate attention and even different statistics than that of instrument reliability. Nevertheless, *there is no reason why the relative and the incremental validity of fully formal measures and of semiformal measures, both having been administered to the same subjects, cannot or should not be considered*. One or the other will prove to be superior in one study or another, but no invidious comparisons need be made.

Both rigorous semi-informal measurement, on the one hand, and content analysis with and without item analysis, on the other hand, are research methods that all researchers should learn to use to one's advantage,[2] depending on the problems and the data they seek to tackle. Researchers may also have their own preferences, with respect to both methods as well as the types of data these methods produce. These *personal methodological preferences (or research styles) should not be confused with a study's ultimate or real reality*. Each of the methods is far from perfection, and to be locked into one or another of them is neither the hallmark of good research nor an informed vote of confidence for the researcher's personally preferred method.

Notes

1. In our experience, the creation of such items is particularly useful with items that receive 50 percent or fewer criterial responses.

2. Our discussion of content analysis in this chapter is intended only for orientational and contrastive purposes (vis-à-vis formal measurement). Before attempting to utilize content analysis (with or without item analysis), the student is strongly advised to read more extensive treatments such as Karl E. Rosengren, ed., *Advances in Content Analysis* (Beverly Hills: Sage, 1981); Robert P. Weber, *Basic Content Analysis* (Newbury Park, CA: Sage, 1990); or Louis A. Gottschalk, *Content Analysis of Verbal Behavior* (Hillsdale, NJ: Erlbaum, 1995).

⟜

What Next? Back to the Future

Depending on the results we obtain from the evaluation of version 2, the steps that are taken thereafter can diverge in a variety of directions. Often enough, the second version is worse than the first insofar as item statistics and instrument reliability are concerned. Such a state of affairs is often attributable to regression toward the mean, an ailment that particularly plagues small sample correlational research and that usually leads to a less than satisfactory validity correlation coefficient. Under such circumstances, it is frequently best to attempt yet a version 3 of the instrument.

Version 3 should not only build on the best items from the first two but should also make every effort to (1) build a longer monodimensional instrument (perhaps also a more monodimensional one than were the first two versions), guided by the substantive implications derived from the best items revealed by the previous versions, (2) obtain a *larger sample* (or samples) of *more varied subjects*, and (3) *increase criterion variance* as much as possible, whether the "two tests–two groups" or the "three tests–one group" validity study design is chosen.[1] If the third version also does not succeed, then a thorough-going reconceptualization of the phenomenon being tested is called for, both at the predictor and at the criterion levels. A substantially different approach, including a search for a better validity criterion, may be the only available option, regardless of how unappealing this may seem.

However, if good fortune has smiled on the researcher, and the test he or she has created seems to be functioning acceptably well vis-à-vis the criterion utilized in version 2, then several options are still available as to next steps. Most researchers will be ready to proceed to the substantive investigations that prompted them to construct their test in the first place. They will want to correlate it with other measures. They will want to see whether it yields significantly different pre- and posttreatment total scores. They will want to find out whether it differentiates between a larger variety of contrasted groups. For instance, if researchers used patients and nonpatients for initial validity purposes, they might now want to compare family members and other caretakers.

In some respects, if researchers undertake a sufficient number of research probes with an instrument that has already been criterion validated, they may now be beginning to suggest or flesh out their test's construct or internal validity as well. Does it correlate negatively with tests that it is supposed to correlate negatively with and positively with tests that it is supposed to correlate positively with? Does it differentiate between groups that it is supposed to and not differentiate between groups that it is not supposed? And do the groups that are supposed to score higher score higher rather than lower? All of the foregoing, and more, yields valuable substantive research utilizing the instrument that has just been created. Moreover, this information also contributes to the better validation and more sensitive appreciation of the instrument itself and of the dimension that it purports to measure.

Devoting Attention to Internal Validity

Now, after the external validity of the test has begun to be satisfactorily demonstrated, the time has arrived for paying ever increasing attention to its internal validity. Now is the time for factor-analytic studies in which the newly created test is investigated in the context of many other similar and dissimilar tests. Now is the time for adding new subdimensions to the test, to see whether they can still be accommodated within a single total score or whether they will need to be handled as separate instruments yielding their own total scores. As the instrument takes on additional and different facets, the researcher's own understanding of the characteristic being tested also undergoes change and becomes richer and more complex. Now may also be the time to see whether semiformal measurement can be fruitfully employed in conjunction with the test to do fuller justice to various more sensitive and intuitive criteria.

The latter task is a particularly important one. Formal measurement provides good ways to get exact, reliable, and valid data on a sizable number of subjects and to do so relatively quickly. But many researchers feel that the very formality or impersonality of formal measurement exacts a price in the extent to which researchers truly know the human beings under study. Similar objections have been raised regarding the capacity of tests to understand human beings even in relation to the very dimension that the test measures. The latter is a familiar criticism directed at schools and educators who rely solely or mostly on standardized test scores to assess students' academic knowledge. The charge that test scores only measure how well students take tests, not what they know, is a somewhat simplistic yet representative articulation of this position. Indeed, some researchers have concluded that the price imposed by formal measurement is just too great. Consequently, they have decided to forego formal measurement as a whole and to use only more dynamic, more intuitive, or more informal methods. They also pay a great price for that decision, because they forego more than precision. There is, after all, also such a thing as "false precision." They forego the self-correction provided by formal measurement's built-in skepticism: the public announcement of the proportion of the criterion variance accounted for by the methods employed.

Fortunately, other researchers refuse to be trapped by all or no methodological decisions. Either on their own or by working together with other researchers, they have attempted to combine various methods that are at various levels of formality and to utilize them in conjunction with criteria that are similarly diversified in this connection. When researchers have finally constructed one or more formal measures that have shown themselves to be satisfactory, the time may have come for the formal measures and the semiformal measures to be utilized together in a joint endeavor to predict one or more criteria of joint interest. Such joint endeavors, in which one takes due care that one method not contaminate the data yielded by the other, can reveal not only the superiority of one method over others to predict an external, clearly measurable criterion, but also the criterial validity of the methods used either alone or together. Any such combination will be more time-consuming than formal measurement alone, even when compared with the time it would take to develop two separate tests for research purposes through the version 3 stage.

Still, the effort involved in using a combined approach for research can be both substantively and methodologically rewarding. Avoidance of contamination between formal and semiformal measurement is easier said than done. Subjects who are aware of being observed or talked to may respond differently to a test than would these or other equivalent subjects who lack such awareness. Similarly, a prior test may influence subsequent behavior, whether observed or merely discussed, though it is unlikely that such experiences will prevail over the long run of informal or semiformal data collection.

Operationalization: A Different Challenge

There is yet another route that can be taken once the validity picture appears to be satisfactory, and that is in the direction of operationalization. Operational tests must face a series of challenges that go considerably beyond any that we have discussed. Operational tests require norms and standardized (i.e., converted) scores. Operational tests must face institutional and public policy scrutiny as to whether measurements along certain dimensions should become part of the record, as well as whether they should be the bases for the differential treatment of students, applicants, patients, customers, among some. Clearly, operational tests face a host of additional hurdles that tests for research purposes do not encounter. For one, the researcher must now consider the professional community or communities that are likely to use the test and respect their shared professional code of ethics. Also, researchers developing an operational test must make their instruments open to the scrutiny and evaluation by fellow researchers regarding the choice of research problem for which the test is intended and the nature of the supporting evidence offered to answer these problems. The operational arena imposes additional codes and evaluations. These additional considerations are essentially social, political, and moral. As such, they are very far from being psychometric alone or, indeed, even from being psychometric primarily.

Nevertheless, good test constructors must not leave operational issues entirely to politicized contenders, nor should they remain innocent babes in the woods regarding the issues that separate these contenders. The considerable expertise of good test constructors must not merely be subject or vulnerable to economic and political parties eager to use "scientific evidence" to advance their own agendas. Hopefully, many test constructors will decide to become informed and skilled researcher-practitioners in conjunction with applied efforts to test individuals so that those individuals can be helped to lead better, fuller, healthier lives.

Researcher-practitioners must take informed and ethical stands on public issues and, in doing so, devote some part of their professional expertise to worthy causes that benefit humans as a species, not only particular sectors of the population. Humans (including researchers) obviously will disagree as to which causes are and are not worthy, particularly since one can never be sure about the eventual outcome of our actions. However, an even greater danger resides in adopting a purportedly neutral or apolitical position. Test constructors must intelligently take sides, while attempting constantly to avoid any semblance of the condemnation that today's older generation has pronounced with respect to the actions and inactions of Hitler's Professors (Weinrich, 1946), for instance. After all, every one of these individuals was a venerable social scientist, from a little more than half a century ago.

Regardless of whether readers choose to proceed either in the operational direction, the internal validity direction or in the joint formal-plus-semiformal testing direction, they must first become familiar with newer and much more advanced methods of test construction. These go far beyond the classical and introductory ones that we have concentrated on in this brief guide.[2]

Notes

1. If the mean of expert ratings is being utilized as the criterion for validating the test that is being created, this can be conceptualized as a variant of the "three test, one group" design. The mean expert ratings constitute the criterion or dependent variable, and these are considered as if they were one test; the researcher's instrument is another, and an already available instrument (previously well validated by other researchers) is the third test. As before, various demographics can also be utilized as additional independent variables or predictors.

2. In recent years, both Sage Publications and Lawrence Erlbaum Publications have developed extensive series pertaining to test construction (as well as to other and often quite different methods). Several of these publications, as well as newer computer programs for item analysis, are listed in the periodic catalogs of the Assessment Systems Corporation (St. Paul, Minnesota).

APPENDIX A

~

Recommended Readings

Basant, K. P. (1996). *Statistics in practice: An illustrated guide to SPSS*. London: Arnold; Pallant, J. (2001). *SPSS survival manual: A step by step guide to data analysis using SPSS for Windows (version 10)*. Buckingham: Open University Press. These are two books particularly useful as resources for students who are not familiar with SPSS. Both books are well organized and present material using accessible yet detailed descriptions and explanations.

Cronbach, L. J. (1990). *Essentials of psychological testing* (5th ed.). New York: HarperCollins. Though this classic text is unfortunately out of print, the reader may wish to invest the effort in obtaining a copy. We find Lee Cronbach's discussion of evaluating a test's criterion validity especially useful and eloquent. Needless to say, chapter 6 is obligatory reading for readers interested in learning more about the Cronbach alpha as a measure of test reliability.

Dawes, R. M., & Smith, T. L. (1985). Attitude and opinion measurement, in G. Lindzey and E. Aronson (Eds.), *The handbook of social psychology* (3rd ed., vol. 1, pp. 509–566). Hillsdale, NJ: Erlbaum. This is a new version of an influential article on attitude research that discusses attitude theory and a number of methodological considerations in attitude research.

Lewis-Beck, M. S. (1980). *Applied regression: An introduction*. Thousand Oaks, CA: Sage. This handy (and short) book provides one of the more accessible explanations on regression that we have come across. The intended audience is similar to that of our book: beginning social researchers, with limited quantitative expertise, who are interested in using regression and related forms of quantitative analyses.

Patten, M. L. (2000). *Understanding research methods* (2nd ed.). Los Angeles: Pyrczak. In "Part D: Measurement," Mildred Patten does a fine job of explaining

validity in its various forms. She also discusses the relationship between validity and reliability and ways to evaluate both. Readers may find the rest of her
book a useful overview to research methods, particularly for those readers interested in a basic, yet accessible introduction.

Peterson, R. A. (1999). *Constructing effective questionnaires*. Thousand Oaks, CA:
Sage. This book presents a more technical approach to instrument construction
than the one we describe in this book, focusing specifically on questionnaires.
However, for the reader who is ready to move on to greater levels of expertise,
Peterson's volume may provide a useful next step. The text includes chapters on
open- and closed-ended questions and on rating scales, as well as on questionnaire structure and evaluation.

Robinson, J. P., Shaver, P. R., & Wrightsman, L. S. (Eds.). (1991). *Measures of personality and social psychological attitudes*. New York: Academic Press. This book
contains an extensive and technical literature on scaling (beyond Likert, Thurstone, and Guttman), which might interest the mathematically advanced
reader. The text focuses on attitude scales, some of which have benefited from
considerable test construction research.

Schuman, H., & Presser, S. (1996). *Questions and answers in attitude surveys*.
Thousand Oaks, CA: Sage; Krebs, D., & Schmidt, P. (Eds.). (1993). *New directions in attitude measurement*. Berlin: de Gruyter. These two books comprise yet
another presentation on scales that is accessible to readers with some basic understanding of tests and test construction.

Stapleton, C. D. (1997). *Basic concepts in exploratory factor analysis (EFA) as a tool
to evaluate score validity: A right-brained approach*. Available: ericae.net/ft/tamu/
Efa.HTM (current as of 8/1/02). This paper presents one of the most accessible
presentations of factor analysis, both exploratory and confirmatory, as pertaining
to tests for research purposes and validity. Though we disagree with Stapleton's
position on the use of exploratory factor analysis for the evaluation of construct
and criterial validity, we still think that readers may find her essay useful.

A P P E N D I X   B

~

Instructions for Performing Necessary Statistical Procedures in SPSS

Recoding Data Entered in Noncriterial Direction

Before attempting any item analysis computations,[1] you must make sure that all item scores are entered in the criterial direction. As you may recall, it is wise to balance a test by reversing the direction of selected items—doing so reduces the possibility of socially desirable (i.e., fake-right) answers. When creating a spreadsheet with the data collected,[2] it is often simpler to enter all responses as marked on test and *then* make the necessary changes for criterial directionality rather than the other way around. What follows are the steps required to ensure that the responses to all the items point in the appropriate direction.

1. From the **SPSS Data Editor** window, use the **Transform** menu and choose **Compute**.
2. Assign a name to the new column that will contain the corrected item scores (e.g., "it1.9crit")[3] in the **Target variable** box.
3. In the **Numeric Expression:** box, enter a minus sign and a left parenthesis; *do not leave a space in between.*
4. Select the item you wish to recode from the list of variables available in the scrollable window on the left and use the ▣ button to place it next to the open parenthesis.
5. Immediately next to the item label (i.e., leave no spaces), enter a minus sign, followed by a whole number. Use the following decision

rules to decide what this number is: If the values you have entered for other items range from 1 to whatever the highest response option is (e.g., 1–4, 1–6, or 1–8), enter a number that is higher by one (i.e., 5, 7, or 9, respectively). If, however, you chose to enter values ranging from 0 to the highest value, enter the highest value. Close the parentheses.

6. The finished formula should resemble the following (where **item1.9** is the variable name):

   (item1.9-5)

   If so, click **OK**.

7. The new variable with the label you chose containing the item's criterial values should have appeared at the right end of the spreadsheet. Remember to use this variable for future analyses. In fact, it may be a good idea to delete the original column and save the spreadsheet with all recoded item responses as a new file. (On **SPSS Data Editor** window, from **File** menu choose **Save as**.)

Calculating Mean Difficulty Scores for Each Item

Before obtaining mean item difficulty scores, all item scores must be coded in the criterial direction (see the prior section). Calculating mean scores is a rather simple procedure that may be performed either in SPSS or in other spreadsheet software (e.g., MS Excel). However, obtaining a histogram for mean scores in SPSS involves a rather complicated set of procedures. We recommend that readers construct the histogram on chart paper after obtaining the mean scores by following these steps:

1. From the **SPSS Data Editor** window, use the **Analyze** menu to select **Reports**. From the options available, choose **Case Summaries**.
2. Select all the items and use the ▣ button to move them to the **Variables** box.
3. Click the **Statistics** button and, from the options available on the next window, choose **Mean**. Click **Continue** and **OK**.
4. The results will be available on the **SPSS Viewer** window. If this window does not appear on its own, it is available from the **Window** menu. Once on this window, click on the **Case Summaries** icon on the navigation bar on the left. The mean scores will be at the bottom of the columns.

5. To print the results, from the **File** menu, choose **Print**. It is also possible to save the results as a text file. From **File** menu, choose **Save As . . . .**

Calculating Item Reliability, Item Validity, and Instrument Reliability Scores

SPSS allows us to calculate alpha-if-item-deleted and corrected item–total correlation item scores as well as the instrument's (Cronbach's) alpha score in a single operation. As with the mean item difficulty scores, it is necessary to have all items coded in the criterial direction before carrying out the calculations (see the first section of this appendix). Similarly, plotting histograms for item reliability and item validity scores involves a set of complicated procedures. Nevertheless, because histograms are quite useful in the evaluation and decision-making process, we recommend that readers draw the histograms by hand on graph paper afterward. Follow these steps to obtain a measure of each item's reliability and validity *and* the instrument's overall reliability:

1. From the **SPSS Data Editor** window, use the **Analyze** menu to select **Scale**. From the options available, choose **Reliability Analysis . . . .**
2. Select all the items and use the ▣ button to move them to the **Items** box.
3. Make sure that next to the **Model:** label **Alpha** is chosen. Click the **Statistics . . .** button.
4. On the next window, under **Descriptives for**, select **Scale if item deleted**. Make sure that all the other options are left unselected and that under **ANOVA Table**, the option **None** is chosen.
5. Click **Continue** and, on the next window, **OK.**
6. The results will be available on the **SPSS Viewer** window. If this window does not appear on its own, it is available from the **Window** menu. Once on this window, click on the **Text Output** icon on the navigation bar on the left. The alpha-if-item-deleted and corrected item–total correlation item scores can be found in columns with their respective headings, under "Item-total Statistics." (Notice that it is quite likely for the columns containing item scores to be split into two groups.) The instrument's Cronbach's alpha score can be found at the bottom of the results.

7. To print the results, from the **File** menu, choose **Print**. It is also possible to save the results as a text file. From **File** menu, choose **Save As . . . .**

Notes

1. The following directions assume that the reader has a basic understanding of SPSS and is able to either enter or import a spreadsheet of the scores for individual tests as well as other relevant data (e.g., demographics and additional independent variables). If the reader is new to SPSS, we suggest that he or she runs the **Tutorial**, which is one of the options available upon launching the program.

2. We assume that the spreadsheets used follow research conventions and are made up of columns containing sets of item response scores (i.e., variables) and corresponding rows with sets of response scores for each subject (i.e., cases). In SPSS, this arrangement would result in labels for each of the test items at the very top and a first row labeled "subject#," for example, with the numbers assigned to each completed test.

3. Note: SPSS does not allow labels that either begin with numbers or that are longer than eight characters.

Sample Data Set of Items and Scores for Self-Esteem Scale, Version 1

Table Appendix C.1. Sample Data Set of Items and Scores for Self-Esteem Scale,* Version 1

Items

A. Global Self-Esteem Dimension	B. Social Self-Esteem Dimension	C. Internal Self-Esteem Dimension
1. I think other people think well of me.	23. Folks listen to me and follow my advice.	37. I don't feel comfortable with groups of strangers.
2. I am popular.	24. Some people admire me.	38. I don't mind being all by myself.
3. I get put down a lot.	25. No one really cares what happens to me.	39. I actually like it better being alone.
4. I think I annoy other people.	26. There are people who see me as a role model.	40. I often feel lonely when I am in groups.
5. I am happy with some things about myself, but I still want to change.	27. What others think of me influences how I see myself.	41. I tend to do a better job when working with others.
6. I often feel self-conscious.	28. Most people have respect for me.	42. As long as others are nearby, I like having my own space.
7. I seem to have a lot of power over others.	29. Others don't care much about what I think.	43. I tend to get depressed when I'm by myself, but feel better when I am with other people.
8. I am often hard on myself.	30. People have told me that I think I'm better than them.	44. I prefer to spend my free time with others rather than alone.
9. I feel that if I apply myself, I succeed.	31. People think I act silly sometimes.	
10. I get along with others easily.		
11. I am satisfied with what I've accomplished in life.		

12. I frequently feel I can't say or do the right thing.
13. I am basically good.
14. I get discouraged easily.
15. I trust that the decisions I make are mostly right.
16. I don't have any challenges in life.
17. I don't feel uncomfortable when people compliment me.
18. I am usually good at finishing jobs quickly.
19. I decide what goes on in my life.
20. I am capable of doing things.
21. Mostly I feel that I'm a burden to others.
22. I have no problem doing things for myself.

32. Other people think I'm interesting.
33. Folks don't think I'm serious enough.
34. People think I have confidence in me.
35. Others take advantage of me.
36. Other people often follow my leadership.

45. I need others to think well of me in order to feel good about myself.
46. I prefer to be left alone.
47. I don't mind if others think I act a little foolish sometimes.
48. I often feel lonely when I'm in a crowd.
49. I need to be told constantly that I'm doing a good job in order to feel good.
50. I spend most of my time alone and I have no problem with that.

(continued)

---

*This scale and the subsequent data set typify those developed and obtained by our students.

Table Appendix C.1. Sample Data Set of Items and Scores for Self-Esteem Scale,* Version 1 (continued)

Subject #	D. Gender	D. White	D. Age	D. Bthord	Item A.1	Item A.2	Item A.3	Item A.4	Item A.5	Item A.6	Item A.7	Item A.8	Item A.9
1	2	2	47	3	2	3	3	3	3	2	2	2	4
2	1	1	42	1	3	2	1	2	3	3	2	2	3
3	2	2	22	2	2	3	3	1	3	3	2	2	4
4	2	2	35	1	3	3	3	4	1	1	2	1	4
5	1	1	46	1	3	3	2	2	2	3	2	2	2
6	2	1	26	2	3	3	2	2	3	3	2	2	4
7	1	1	33	1	3	2	1	2	1	2	3	2	3
8	2	1	33	1	3	2	2	4	4	2	2	2	3
9	1	2	42	3	3	4	1	1	3	2	2	3	2
10	1	1	44	4	4	4	1	4	1	3	4	1	4
11	2	2	44	2	4	3	1	3	2	1	3	3	4
12	2	1	31	3	3	3	1	4	3	2	3	2	3
13	2	2	48	3	2	2	1	2	3	2	3	1	3
14	1	2	48	2	4	3	1	2	1	1	2	1	4
15	2	2	43	3	3	3	2	2	3	2	2	3	3
16	1	1	22	1	4	3	1	4	2	2	2	1	4
17	1	1	24	1	4	3	2	4	3	2	3	3	3
18	1	1	35	2	3	2	2	3	1	2	3	3	4
19	1	1	26	3	4	3	1	2	2	2	2	1	4
20	1	1	32	3	4	4	2	4	3	1	2	2	4

ID													
21	1	1	54	3	3	2	1	1	1	1	2	2	2
22	1	2	37	2	2	2	3	4	2	3	3	3	4
23	2	1	55	4	2	1	4	1	1	3	1	4	2
24	2	2	48	2	2	2	2	2	2	1	2	3	2
25	1	2	35	4	3	2	2	2	3	2	2	2	1
26	2	1	55	1	4	1	2	4	1	3	2	2	3
27	1	2	31	4	3	3	3	1	2	2	2	1	3
28	2	1	32	3	3	2	1	2	3	3	3	2	2
29	2	2	39	2	4	2	1	2	2	3	2	3	2
30	1	2	42	3	3	3	2	2	2	3	3	2	2
31	2	1	58	3	4	3	1	3	1	2	2	3	4
32	1	2	47	3	4	3	2	2	2	3	3	2	3
33	2	1	47	1	2	3	1	3	1	3	2	3	2
34	1	2	37	1	3	2	1	2	2	3	2	3	2
35	1	1	58	1	2	2	1	1	3	3	2	2	2
36	1	1	38	4	3	2	1	2	2	3	2	2	3
37	1	1	34	3	3	3	3	1	1	2	2	1	3
38	2	2	34	2	3	3	1	2	2	3	3	2	2
39	2	2	37	3	4	2	1	2	2	3	2	3	2
40	1	1	39	3	4	3	1	3	3	3	2	2	3

Note: Item scores are as recorded on test (i.e. recoding in the criterial direction may be necessary for some). Codes for demographic items (i.e., column labels beginning with D.) are as follows: *Gender:* 1=male/2=female; *White:* 1=White/2 =Non-White; *Birth Order:* 4=only child/3=eldest/2=middle/1=youngest. (Birth order scoring reflects a progression from least to most family resources, which itself is hypothesized to influence self-esteem.) Likert scale scores for items A.1–C.50 (i.e., *Self-Esteem Scale*) are as follows: 1=Never True/2=Sometimes True/3=Often True/4=Usually True.

(continued)

Table Appendix C.1. Sample Data Set of Items and Scores for Self-Esteem Scale,* Version 1 (continued)

Item A.10	Item A.11	Item A.12	Item A.13	Item A.14	Item A.15	Item A.16	Item A.17	Item A.18	Item A.19	Item A.20	Item A.21	Item A.22	Item B.23
4	1	1	4	3	3	2	2	3	2	2	3	3	3
2	1	1	4	4	3	2	3	3	2	4	3	3	4
3	2	2	3	4	3	3	3	3	3	3	3	4	4
3	1	1	4	3	3	2	4	4	4	4	4	4	3
3	2	2	4	3	2	2	2	2	2	2	2	2	2
3	2	2	4	3	3	2	2	2	3	3	3	4	4
2	2	3	2	4	1	2	2	2	4	2	2	2	3
2	1	2	4	3	3	1	3	3	3	4	4	4	4
3	2	3	2	3	3	2	2	3	2	2	3	3	2
4	1	1	4	4	3	3	4	4	4	4	4	4	4
4	1	4	4	3	2	2	2	3	1	3	3	3	4
3	2	1	4	3	3	3	4	3	2	4	4	3	2
4	2	2	4	3	3	1	2	4	4	3	3	3	3
4	2	2	4	4	3	2	4	3	4	4	4	3	4
3	1	1	4	2	3	3	4	4	2	3	4	3	3
3	1	1	4	4	4	3	4	4	4	4	4	3	3
3	2	2	4	4	3	1	3	4	3	3	4	4	3
3	1	2	3	3	3	2	3	3	2	3	3	3	4
4	1	1	4	4	4	3	3	4	4	4	4	4	4
3	2	1	4	4	3	1	3	3	3	4	4	4	2

2	2	3	2	3	2	2	2	2	2	3	2	2
4	3	4	3	3	3	1	2	2	4	3	4	4
1	4	4	2	1	1	1	1	1	1	1	1	1
2	2	2	2	2	2	2	3	2	2	2	2	2
3	2	3	2	2	3	3	4	3	4	3	3	3
2	2	4	3	3	3	3	2	2	3	2	2	2
3	1	3	2	4	4	3	3	4	3	3	3	3
2	2	2	2	3	3	2	3	3	2	2	2	2
2	2	2	3	3	3	2	2	3	2	2	2	2
2	2	4	3	3	3	2	2	2	2	1	2	2
2	2	3	4	2	2	2	2	1	3	4	3	2
2	2	2	3	3	3	3	3	2	2	3	3	4
3	2	4	3	3	3	2	2	3	2	3	3	3
3	3	3	4	2	3	3	3	2	3	2	2	3
1	2	1	2	3	3	3	2	3	2	3	3	3
2	2	4	3	2	3	2	2	2	2	2	2	2
1	3	2	2	3	2	3	3	2	3	3	3	3
3	1	3	4	2	3	2	2	4	3	2	2	2
2	2	2	2	2	2	3	2	3	2	2	2	2
2	2	2	3	3	2	2	3	2	2	2	2	2
3	1	4	3	3	3	3	3	3	3	3	3	3

Note: Item scores are as recorded on test (i.e. recoding in the criterial direction may be necessary for some). Codes for demographic items (i.e., column labels beginning with D.) are as follows: *Gender:* 1=male/2=female; *White:* 1=White/2 =Non-White; *Birth Order:* 4=only child/3=eldest/2=middle/1=youngest. (Birth order scoring reflects a progression from least to most family resources, which itself is hypothesized to influence self-esteem.) Likert scale scores for items A.1–C.50 (i.e., *Self-Esteem Scale*) are as follows: 1=Never True/2=Sometimes True/3=Often True/4=Usually True.

(continued)

Table Appendix C.1. Sample Data Set of Items and Scores for Self-Esteem Scale,* Version 1 (continued)

Item B.24	Item B.25	Item B.26	Item B.27	Item B.28	Item B.29	Item B.30	Item B.31	Item B.32	Item B.33	Item B.34	Item B.35	Item B.36	Item C.37
4	2	2	2	4	2	3	2	4	1	2	2	1	1
3	2	3	3	3	2	3	2	2	3	2	2	3	3
3	2	3	3	3	2	2	3	3	2	3	2	3	2
4	2	3	4	4	2	4	3	4	1	3	1	4	4
3	2	2	3	3	2	3	2	2	2	2	2	3	4
4	2	2	2	3	3	3	2	2	2	3	2	3	4
3	2	2	3	2	2	3	2	3	3	2	4	2	3
4	2	2	3	3	2	2	4	3	1	3	2	4	4
4	2	2	2	3	2	2	3	3	2	2	1	4	1
4	2	3	4	4	4	4	4	1	2	4	1	3	1
4	4	4	4	4	4	4	4	4	1	3	1	4	3
4	2	3	3	3	2	3	2	2	4	3	2	2	4
4	3	3	3	4	3	3	4	4	1	4	2	4	1
4	4	4	4	2	3	4	2	2	4	4	2	4	1
4	2	3	3	4	3	3	4	3	2	3	1	4	4
4	2	2	4	4	3	3	3	3	1	3	1	3	4
4	3	3	3	4	3	3	3	3	1	3	1	3	4
3	2	2	2	4	2	2	2	2	2	2	2	3	4
4	4	4	4	4	2	4	4	4	2	4	3	3	4
4	3	2	3	3	2	3	3	2	2	3	2	3	1

3	2	2	2	3	2	3	2	2	4	2	1	3
4	4	3	4	4	2	3	4	2	2	3	2	2
3	1	2	1	1	1	1	1	2	4	2	1	2
3	2	2	2	2	2	2	2	2	2	2	3	2
3	3	2	3	2	2	3	3	3	3	3	2	3
2	2	2	2	3	1	3	3	1	2	2	1	4
4	2	2	2	4	2	3	3	2	2	2	1	2
3	2	2	2	3	2	2	2	2	1	2	2	1
3	2	2	2	2	1	2	2	2	2	2	2	4
2	2	2	2	2	2	2	3	3	3	2	2	4
3	4	4	4	3	3	3	3	2	2	2	2	2
3	2	2	2	4	2	2	2	2	3	2	2	1
3	2	2	2	3	2	3	3	2	2	2	2	4
4	3	2	3	2	2	3	3	2	2	3	3	4
3	1	2	1	3	2	3	3	2	3	2	2	4
4	3	2	3	2	2	3	3	2	3	2	3	1
4	2	2	2	4	2	3	3	2	3	2	2	4
3	2	2	2	3	1	2	2	2	2	2	2	4
3	2	2	2	2	2	2	2	2	2	2	2	4

Note: Item scores are as recorded on test (i.e. recoding in the criterial direction may be necessary for some). Codes for demographic items (i.e., column labels beginning with D.) are as follows: *Gender:* 1=male/2=female; *White:* 1=White/2 =Non-White; *Birth Order:* 4=only child/3=eldest/2=middle/1=youngest. (Birth order scoring reflects a progression from least to most family resources, which itself is hypothesized to influence self-esteem.) Likert scale scores for items A.1–C.50 (i.e., *Self-Esteem Scale*) are as follows: 1=Never True/2=Sometimes True/3=Often True/4=Usually True.

(continued)

Table Appendix C.1. Sample Data Set of Items and Scores for Self-Esteem Scale,* Version 1 (*continued*)

Item C.38	Item C.39	Item C.40	Item C.41	Item C.42	Item C.43	Item C.44	Item C.45	Item C.46	Item C.47	Item C.48	Item C.49	Item C.50
1	2	2	3	4	2	3	2	4	4	3	1	1
4	1	2	4	4	1	4	2	2	4	2	1	1
4	1	3	3	2	4	3	2	2	3	3	1	2
4	1	4	4	4	1	3	1	4	4	4	1	1
3	2	2	2	4	3	3	2	2	3	2	2	3
3	2	2	4	3	4	3	1	4	4	2	1	2
3	2	2	3	3	2	3	2	2	2	2	2	2
4	2	2	4	4	3	3	1	3	4	4	1	1
3	3	3	4	3	4	3	2	3	3	2	2	1
4	1	4	4	4	3	4	1	4	4	4	1	1
4	1	4	4	4	1	3	3	3	3	1	2	3
4	2	2	3	4	2	4	1	2	4	4	1	2
4	2	2	4	4	2	3	1	4	3	2	1	1
3	3	3	3	4	4	4	1	4	4	4	2	1
4	1	3	4	4	3	4	1	4	4	4	1	1
4	1	3	4	4	1	4	1	3	4	4	1	2
3	2	4	3	3	3	3	3	2	3	2	2	1
4	1	2	4	3	4	3	1	3	4	3	1	2

3	2	3	3	2	3	2	3	2	3	3	1	2	2
4	3	1	4	3	4	3	4	1	4	4	1	2	1
2	1	3	1	1	2	4	2	4	2	1	1	4	4
2	2	3	2	2	2	2	2	2	2	3	2	2	2
3	1	3	1	3	3	3	3	1	2	3	1	2	2
4	2	2	2	2	4	4	4	1	3	4	3	1	2
3	2	3	4	3	3	2	3	2	3	3	3	2	1
2	3	3	3	2	3	4	3	2	3	3	2	2	2
1	2	3	1	2	3	3	3	2	2	3	1	2	3
4	2	1	2	2	4	2	4	2	2	4	1	2	2
4	4	1	3	2	3	2	3	2	3	3	3	1	2
3	2	3	3	3	3	3	3	2	3	3	2	1	2
2	2	3	3	3	3	4	3	3	3	3	2	2	1
3	1	3	2	1	2	3	2	3	2	2	2	2	3
2	1	3	2	2	3	4	3	3	2	2	2	2	2
3	1	3	2	2	3	2	3	2	3	2	2	2	3
3	2	2	4	2	2	2	2	2	3	3	2	2	1
3	2	3	3	2	3	2	3	3	3	3	3	2	2
2	2	2	1	2	3	2	3	2	2	3	2	2	2
1	2	3	3	2	4	4	4	2	3	3	1	2	3
3	2	3	3	2	3	4	3	2	3	3	2	1	2

Note: Item scores are as recorded on test (i.e. recoding in the criterial direction may be necessary for some). Codes for demographic items (i.e., column labels beginning with D.) are as follows: *Gender:* 1=male/2=female; *White:* 1=White/2 =Non-White; *Birth Order:* 4=only child/3=eldest/2=middle/1=youngest. (Birth order scoring reflects a progression from least to most family resources, which itself is hypothesized to influence self-esteem.) Likert scale scores for items A.1–C.50 (i.e., *Self-Esteem Scale*) are as follows: 1=Never True/2=Sometimes True/3=Often True/4=Usually True.

References

Adorno, T. W., Frenkel-Brunswik, E., Levinson, D. J., & Sanford, R. N. (1993). *The authoritarian personality*. New York: Norton.

Allport, G. W., Vernon, P. E., & Gardner, L. (1970). *Study of values*. Chicago: Riverside.

Beck, A. T., Weissman, A., Lester, D., & Trexler, L. (1974). The measurement of pessimism: The Hopelessness Scale. *Journal of Consulting and Clinical Psychology, 42*(6), 861–865.

Billings, A. G., & Moos, R. H. (1981). The role of coping responses and social resources in attenuating the stress of life events. *Journal of Behavioral Medicine, 4*, 139–157.

Cronbach, L. J. (1990). *Essentials of psychological testing* (5th ed.). New York: HarperCollins.

Dawes, R. M., & Smith, T. L. (1985). Attitude and opinion measurement. In G. Lindzey & E. Aronson (Eds.), *The handbook of social psychology* (3rd. ed., vol. 1, pp. 509–566). Hillsdale, NJ: Erlbaum.

Dunst, C. J., Trivette, C. M., & Deal, A. G. (1988). *Enabling and empowering families: Principles and guidelines for practice*. Cambridge, MA: Brookline.

Fishman, J. A. (1955). Negative stereotypes concerning Americans among American-born children receiving various types of minority-group education. *Genetic Psychology Monographs, 51*, 107–182.

Fishman, J. A., & Lorge, (1954). The role of the culture-group affiliation of the "judge" in Thurstone attitude scale construction. *American Psychologist, 9*, 368–369.

Fishman, J. A., et al. (1964). Guidelines for testing minority-group children. *Journal of social issues, 20*(2), 129–145.

Fowler, F. J., Jr. (1993). *Survey research methods.* Newbury Park, CA: Sage.

Gottschalk, L. A. (1995). *Content analysis of verbal behavior.* Hillsdale: Erlbaum.

Guilford, J. P. (1956). Correction in *r* for errors of grouping. In *Fundamental statistics in psychology and education* (pp. 329–331). New York: McGraw-Hill.

Guttman, L. (1950). The basis for scalogram analysis. In S. Stouffer et al. (Eds.), *Measurement and prediction.* Princeton, NJ: Princeton University Press.

Henerson, M. E., Morris, L. L., & Fitz-Gibbons, C. T. (1987). *How to measure attitudes.* Newbury Park, CA: Sage.

Hudson, W. W. (1982). *The clinical measurement package: A field manual.* Homewood, IL: Dorsey.

Karl E. Rosengren (Ed.). (1981). *Advances in content analysis.* Beverly Hills: Sage.

Krebs, D., & Schmidt, P. (1993). (Eds.). *New directions in attitude measurement.* Berlin: de Gruyter.

Lewis-Beck, M. S. (1980). *Applied regression: An introduction.* Thousand Oaks, CA: Sage.

Likert, R. (1932). *A technique for the measurement of attitudes.* New York: McGraw-Hill.

Patten, M. L. (2000). *Understanding research methods* (2nd ed.). Los Angeles: Pyrczak.

Peterson, R. A. (1999). *Constructing effective questionnaires.* Thousand Oaks: Sage.

Robinson, J. P., Shaver, P. R., & Wrightsman, L. S. (Eds.). (1991). *Measures of personality and social psychological attitudes.* New York: Academic Press.

Rotter, J. B., & Rafferty, J. E. (1950). *The Rotter incomplete sentences blank manual: College form.* New York: Psychological Corporation.

Rosengren, K. E. (1981). *Advances in content analysis.* Beverly Hills, CA: Sage.

Schuman, H., & Presser, S. (1996). *Questions and answers in attitude surveys.* Thousand Oaks, CA: Sage.

Singleton, R. A., Jr., Straits, B. C., & Straits, M. M. (1993). *Approaches to social research* (2nd ed.). New York: Oxford University Press.

Snider, J. G., & Osgood, C. E. (1969). *Semantic differential technique.* Chicago: Aldine.

Stouthamer-Loeber, M., & van Kammen, W. B. (1995). *Data collection and management: A practical guide.* Newbury Park, CA: Sage.

Stappleton, C. D. (1997). *Basic concepts in exploratory factor analysis (EFA) as a tool to evaluate score validity: A right-brained approach.* Available: ericae.net/ft/tamu/Efa.HTM

Thurstone, L. (1929). Theory of attitude measurement. *Psychological Bulletin, 36,* 222–241.

Thurstone, L., & Chave, E. J. (1929). *The measurement of attitudes.* Chicago: University of Chicago Press.

Weber, R. P. (1990). *Basic content analysis.* Newbury Park, CA: Sage.

Weinreich, M. (1946). *Hitler's Professors.* New York: Yiddish Scientific Institute (YIVO).

Index

Adorno, Theodor, 123
aesthetic considerations, 96
alchemy, 12, 127
Allport-Vernon Scale of Values, 88
alpha values, 58, 60
alpha-if-item-deleted scores, 58, 60,
    62, 108, 116, 145
alternate-forms reliability, 27
answering behaviors, 86–87

Beck Hopelessness Scale (Beck),
    124–25
bell-shaped curve. See normal
    distribution
biserial correlations, 49n4, 64
Bureau of Standard Weights and
    Measures, 21, 38

causation, 30
children, 127–28
closed instruments, 97, 131–32
coding, 105
coefficient, 27, 29. See also correlation
    coefficient

collaboration, 89, 137
commercially available tests, 7
componentiality, 82–86; factor
    analysis, 85–86; unitary underlying
    phenomenon, 84
computerized statistical packages. See
    statistical packages
conceptual validity, 110
concurrent validity, 20
consensually contrasted groups, 41–43,
    49n2, 82
consistency, 22. See also item
    consistency
construct validity, 19–20, 22, 77, 91,
    105; first version of test, 91
content analysis, 5, 78, 128–30, 134n2
content validity, 19, 20, 91
continuous scoring, 53–54, 60, 64,
    97–99
control, 1
Coping Scale (Billings and Moos), 46,
    121, 122
corrected item total correlation. See
    item discriminability

correlation, 28, 46, 49n1, 82, 125n1;
  infinite regress, 40–41; multiple,
  121, 125n1
correlation coefficient, 23, 24nn1, 2,
  28–31, 49n4, 68n2; Pearson
  product moment correlation
  coefficient, 28–29, 31, 33n1, 49n4,
  60, 113; statistical significance,
  30–31
criterial direction, 53–55, 97–99, 105
criterion validity, 4–5, 19, 35–38, 63,
  91; analyzing second version, 115,
  121–25; consensually contrasted
  groups, 41–43, 49n2; demographic
  characteristics to increase criterial
  predictions, 46–49; expert opinion
  and, 39–40; previously well-
  validated tests, 40–41;
  responsibility of researcher, 36–37;
  simple and unforced stepwise
  regression, 43–44. See also external
  criterion; external validity
Cronbach's alpha score, 28, 145
cross-method contamination, 15–16
cutoff scores, 32

decision sheets, 107, 108, 109–10,
  120
degree of criteriality, 53
demographic variables, 46–49, 84,
  124; first version of test, 91–92,
  97–98; second version of test, 121,
  124
dependent variable, 43–44
dichotomous scoring, 53, 60, 64,
  97–99
differentiation, 41–43, 45
distribution of scores, 54–56, 62; item
  discriminability and, 64–55

empirical considerations, 1–3, 35–36
empirical validity, 110

ethics, 138–39
examinations, 12
examples: attitudes toward government
  spending, 42–43; basketball success,
  29, 88; bathroom scale, 21, 22, 25,
  31; blood pressure example, 38;
  Caregiver Questionnaire (Adachi),
  46–47, 47, 124; English-only
  legislation, 83–85, 96–97, 102,
  123–24; Fear of Cancer Self-
  Screening Test (Perry), 54–56, 55,
  60–62, 61, 65, 67, 68n1, 106–8,
  107, 112; height and weight
  correlation, 84–85; helplessness,
  124–25; intelligence, 30, 31, 83;
  Medical Coping Index (Martin),
  45–46, 57, 58, 59, 62, 65, 66, 67,
  68n1, 83–85, 96, 97, 99–100, 108,
  109–10, 111, 112; Medical Coping
  Index II (MCI II) (Martin), 116–21,
  117–20, 121–23; negative
  stereotypes, 11; personality construct
  example, 41; PSDI, 46–47; reading
  difficulties, 102; readings of
  Shakespeare, 130; SAT scores, 30,
  31, 84–85; seesaw, 29; spelling test,
  53, 70; study skills example, 37–38;
  Test Anxiety Survey, 45; voting
  behavior examples, 98
expert opinion, 39–40, 63, 82, 139n1
explanatory considerations, 16–17, 122
external criterion, 2, 4, 35–38, 79. See
  also criterion validity; external
  validity
external validity, 1–2, 19–24, 91;
  importance of, 22–24; instrument
  design and, 81–82. See also
  criterion validity; external criterion

face validity, 19, 20
factor analysis, 85–86, 90n1, 136
false precision, 137

Family Support Scale (Dunst), 124
Fechner, Gustave, 71
Federal Office Of Management and
   Budget, 96
field observations, 129
first version of test, 5, 79; criterial
   direction, 97–99; demographic
   variables, 91–92, 97–98; formal
   evaluation, 77–78; formatting of
   items, 77; instrument format, 93,
   96–97; item analyses, 106–11; item
   consistency, 105, 106–7; item
   difficulty, 105; item discriminability,
   105–7; item pool, 93–100; pilot-
   testing, 77, 100–104; reliability,
   111–13; researcher's log, 92–93;
   sample selection, 91–92; scales, 92;
   subdimensions, 93, 97, 99–100,
   108. See also second version of test
formal measurement, 13–17, 35, 127;
   compared with semiformal
   measurement, 132–33; limitations,
   136–37. See also semiformal
   measurement
format, 77, 79, 96–97
F-Scale, 123–24

Galton, Francis, 43, 112
Generalized Contentment Scale
   (GCS) (Hudson), 45–46, 46, 121
Guttman, Louis, 74
Guttman scaling, 5, 74–76

Hitler's Professors, 139
homogeneity of tests, 26, 56

implicational/scalable tasks, 74, 75
Implicit Antidemocratic Trends of
   Potentiality for Fascism Scale (F-
   Scale), 123–24
incremental validity, 44–46, 48–49,
   82, 122

independent variable, 43–44
infinite regress, 40–41
instrument design: componentiality,
   82–86; external validity, 81–82;
   instrument length, 96, 103, 135;
   item characteristics, 86–90;
   literature review, 82–83;
   open/closed instruments, 99,
   131–32; response variance, 87–89,
   90n3; terminology, 102–3; title for
   test, 96–97. See also first version of
   test; second version of test; tests
interitem consistency (reliability),
   60–64, 73, 79, 106–7, 116
internal validity, 19, 21–22, 122,
   136–38
interrater reliability, 31–32
interval level of measurement, 14
interview schedules, 130–31
ipsativity, 77, 87–88, 90n2
item analyses, 5, 51–52, 106–11,
   115–21; decision sheets, 107, 108,
   109–10; factor analysis, 85–86,
   90n1, 136; item consistency, 52,
   56–63; item difficulty, 52–56; item
   discriminability, 52, 63–67;
   semiformal measurement, 128–30
item bias, 86–87, 94
item characteristics, 86–90; content
   characteristics, 86–87; response
   variance, 87–89, 90n3
item consistency (reliability), 5,
   56–63, 79; analyzing first version,
   105, 106–7; analyzing second
   version, 116, 118; if item deleted,
   58–60; interitem consistency,
   60–64, 68n2, 73, 79, 106–7, 116
item difficulty, 5, 52–56, 79, 105, 116,
   117; calculating, 144–45
item discriminability, 5, 63–67;
   analyzing first version, 105–7;
   analyzing second version, 116, 119

item pool: first version of test, 93–100; questions to ask, 93–95; semantic differential scale, 98–99
item scalability, 75
item statistics, 115–21
item-related error variance, 27
items: dichotomous/continuous, 53, 60, 64, 89, 97–99; formal evaluation of, 77–78; preestablished, 130–31

judges, 72–73

Kuder-Richardson correlation, 28

Lewin, Kurt, 78
Likert, Renis, 70
Likert scaling, 5, 69–71, 73, 76, 82, 90n3
linear regression equation, 43–44
linear relationship, 82
literature review, 20–21, 63, 79, 82–83, 122

measurement. See formal measurement; semiformal measurement
median interitem consistency, 68n2, 106–7
monodimensional instrument, 135
multiple correlation, 121, 125n1
multiple-regression analysis, 43–44
multiple-test approach, 78, 85

n values, 58
nominal level of measurement, 13
no-response answers, 30
normal distribution, 54, 62, 105, 116
null hypothesis, 30

objectivity, 1
one-group, three-test paradigm, 48, 121

one-total-score approach, 86
open instruments, 99, 131–32
operational tests, 6, 14, 32–33, 92, 122, 124, 138–39
opinion surveys, 123–24
ordinal measurement, 13, 14

participant observation, 129
Pearson product moment correlation coefficient, 28–29, 31, 33n1, 49n4, 60, 113
Pearsonian r, 64, 65, 66, 67
Perceived Support Inventory (PSI-2), 124
percentile scores, 14
personal methodological preferences, 133
phenomenon (real thing), 1, 2, 63, 81, 84; validity and, 36–37
phi correlation, 60
pilot-testing, 77, 79, 91–92, 100–104
plan of book, 2–7
predictive validity, 19
preestablished items, 130–31
previously validated tests, 40–41, 46–47, 82, 121–22, 130, 137–38
probability, 16, 30, 32–33
professional community, 138
projective techniques, 129–30

Q-sort instruments, 88, 90n2
qualitative research, 22
questionnaire approach, 85

R^2, 44
r^2, 44
raters, 31–32, 39–40, 63, 133
rating scales, 130–31
ratio level of measurement, 14
readability, 86, 102
real thing. See phenomenon
realities, external, 23

recommended readings, 141–42
regression, 33n1, 46, 82; infinite
   regress, 40–41; stepwise, 43–45, 48,
   125; zero-order, 44, 45
regression equation, 43–44
regression toward the mean, 43,
   112–13, 135
"Regression towards Mediocrity in
   Hereditary Stature" (Galton), 43
reliability, 4, 5, 22, 73, 79; analyzing
   first version, 111–13; analyzing
   second version, 115–21;
   determining, 27–28; error variance
   and, 25–27; interrater, 31–32;
   logical and operational
   implications of, 31–33; score
   variance and, 29–30; as upper limit
   of validity, 31, 37, 92. See also
   correlation coefficient; item
   consistency; validity
reliability correlations, 49n1
research styles, 133
research traditions, 38
researcher, 15, 127; responsibility of,
   36–37
researcher involvement. See
   semiformal measurement
researcher-practitioners, 138–39
researcher's log, 80, 92–93, 122
Rotter's Sentence Completion Test, 132
rough grouping, 60, 62, 64, 116

sample data set, 6, 147–57
scales. See Sociopsychological scales
scientific process, 1
score constancy, 56
scores, 14; alpha-if-item-deleted, 58,
   60, 62, 116, 145; Cronbach's alpha,
   28, 145; dichotomous/continuous,
   54–56, 60, 62, 64–65, 97–99;
   standardized, 137, 138; total, 64,
   73, 78, 84, 86, 136

scoring manuals, 131, 132, 133
second version of test, 79, 108, 112;
   criterion validity, 115, 121–25;
   demographic variables, 121, 124;
   item statistics and instrument
   reliability, 115–21
self-conviction, 22
self-criticism, 17
Self-Esteem Scale, 147–57
SEm (standard error of measurement),
   32
semantic differential scale, 98–99,
   104n2
semiformal measurement, 5, 78,
   127–28, 136–37; compared with
   formal measurement, 132–33; open
   vs. closed instruments, 131–32;
   two-dimensional grid, 128–32. See
   also formal measurement
social policy, 48, 124, 138–39
sociopsychological scales, 69;
   Guttman scaling, 5, 74–76; judges,
   72–73; Likert scaling, 5, 69–71, 73,
   76, 82, 90n3; Thurstone scaling, 5,
   71–74, 76
SPSS, 44, 58, 64, 111–12;
   instructions, 143–46
squared regression coefficient, 33n1
standard deviation, 32
standard error of measurement (SEm),
   32
standardized test scores, 137, 138
statistical packages, 8, 43–44, 49n4,
   58; analyzing first version, 111–12
statistical significance, 30–31
statistics, 7. See also correlation
   coefficient
Stephenson, William, 90n2
stepwise regression, 43–45, 48, 125
subdimensions of tests, 26, 49, 136;
   first version of test, 93, 97, 105,
   108; validity and, 110–11

subject bias, 112
subjects, 7–8; answering behaviors,
    20–21, 86–87, 94; children,
    127–28; consensually contrasted
    groups, 41–43, 49n2, 82; debriefing
    sessions, 101–2; error variance and,
    25–26; first version of test and,
    91–92, 100–103; influences on,
    137–38; sample size, 12, 135

terminology, 94, 102–3
test–retest reliability, 27
tests: cost considerations, 27, 36, 39,
    40, 78, 116; defined, xii, 12;
    homogeneity of, 26, 56; multiple
    versions, 78, 85; previously
    validated, 40–41, 46–47, 82,
    121–22, 130, 137–38; for research
    purposes, 11–13; separation and
    independence, 15–16; titles, 96–97.
    See also first version of test;
    instrument design; second version
    of test; subdimensions of tests
tetrachoric correlation, 60
theoretical considerations, 3, 35–36,
    48, 78, 108
third version of test, 78, 122, 135
three tests–one group design, 135
Thurstone, Louis, 71
Thurstone scaling, 5, 71–74, 76
time-related error variance, 27
title for test, 96–97

total score, 64, 73, 78, 84, 86, 136
transformed scores, 14
transparency, 20, 21
two-dimensional grid, 128–32
two-group, two-test paradigm, 48, 121,
    135
two-pronged questions, 94

unitary underlying phenomenon, 84

validity, 4; conceptual, 110; concurrent,
    20; construct, 19–20, 22, 77, 91,
    105; content, 19, 20, 91; direct *vs.*
    indirect indicators, 21; external, 1–2,
    19–20, 22–24, 81–82, 91; face, 19,
    20; first version of test, 91;
    incremental, 44–46, 48–49, 82, 122;
    internal, 19, 21–22, 122, 136–38;
    literature review and, 20–21;
    phenomenon and, 36–37; predictive,
    19; reliability as upper limit of, 31,
    37, 92; subdimensions of test and,
    110–11; as ultimate goal, 19, 81. *See*
    also criterion validity; external
    criterion; reliability
variables, 43–44. *See also* demographic
    variables
variance, 25–27, 29–30, 38, 71, 135;
    item characteristics, 87–89, 90n3

zero-order correlation, 125n1
zero-order regression, 44, 45

~

About the Authors

Joshua A. Fishman is distinguished university professor emeritus in social sciences at Yeshiva University, and visiting professor in linguistics and education at Stanford University, in multiculturism at New York University, and in linguistics at CUNY Graduate Center. He was formerly director of research for the CEEB and has taught (and continues to teach) courses in "Test Construction for Research Purposes" throughout the world. This student-oriented book is largely a by-product of his efforts to make test construction "learner-friendly." His most recent book (2001) is *Can Threatened Languages Be Saved?* Dr. Fishman received his Ph.D. in social psychology from Columbia University in 1953.

Tomás Galguera is associate professor in the Teachers for Tomorrow's Schools teacher education program at Mills College, where he teaches in and coordinates the cross-cultural language and academic development emphasis component of the program. Dr. Galguera is a fellow at the Carnegie Academy for Scholarship of Teaching and Learning. He received his Ph.D. from Stanford University and has published articles in *The Multilingual Educator*, *Language Learning* and the *Hispanic Journal of Behavioral Sciences*. His current research interests include the preparation of teachers of language minority students and the use of video for instructional, documentation, and assessment purposes.